Anonymous

The North Carolina Practical Spelling-Book

A Complete Graded Course in Orthography for the Use of Public and Private

Schools

Anonymous

The North Carolina Practical Spelling-Book
A Complete Graded Course in Orthography for the Use of Public and Private Schools

ISBN/EAN: 9783337778989

Printed in Europe, USA, Canada, Australia, Japan

Cover: Foto ©Thomas Meinert / pixelio.de

More available books at **www.hansebooks.com**

NORTH CAROLINA SERIES.

THE

NORTH CAROLINA

PRACTICAL SPELLING-BOOK:

A COMPLETE GRADED COURSE IN ORTHOGRAPHY

FOR THE USE OF

PUBLIC AND PRIVATE SCHOOLS.

COMPILED BY A NORTH CAROLINA TEACHER.

RALEIGH, N. C.:
ALFRED WILLIAMS & COMPANY.
1892.

PREFACE.

This book is prepared for the public and private schools of North Carolina, and it is the result of long and careful study of the needs of our educational systems. It is believed that it will be found to be the very best book of its kind for the particular place which it is intended to occupy in the schools of our State.

The distinctively local features will be especially valuable to the children of our State, as they give necessary instruction which has heretofore been unattainable with anything like accuracy.

We desire to acknowledge special obligation to Dr. Joseph A. Holmes, State Geologist, for kind assistance in preparing correct lists of minerals, trees, shrubs and flora of North Carolina.

This book does not pretend to contain every word in our language, but it claims to set forth an actual and practical vocabulary of words generally used by Americans in speaking and writing; and as a practical spelling-book for children it is submitted to North Carolina teachers for their approval.   THE AUTHOR.

Raleigh, N. C., September 1, 1892.

A FEW WORDS WITH THE TEACHER.

In orthoepy we have endeavored to adhere to the principles of common sense, adopting as authority the usage of the best American writers and speakers of our language. In cases where words have two or more authorized pronunciations preference is here given to that in most general use among the educated people of the Southern States.

The orthography is that of Webster's New International Dictionary, which is considered the standard for American people.

This book is not intended for a primer or a reader, neither is it an encyclopedia or a dictionary, but it is so complete and carefully graded that it may be used by all ages of pupils from the primary to the most advanced.

Spelling is to be learned almost entirely by memory, and set rules are of very little use, there being so many "exceptions"; hence all rules are omitted here. A word is a combination of letters to express an idea, and that combination is more often arbitrary than the result of a rule.

Teaching a child to spell correctly is the hardest work of the teacher, but it is one of the most essential parts of an education, "bad spelling" being everywhere considered an evidence of a lack of culture.

In order to thoroughly fix in the memory the orthography of our language there should be, in addition to the regular lessons herein arranged, other frequent practice with the pupils in dictation. Such exercises may be taken from various sources, and the newspapers or magazines will be found exceedingly helpful, as they contain the words of most practical and general use in the literature of the times.

No definitions of words are here given, because the most important thing with pupils is to know the orthography of the word, for the definitions will be learned in due time as occasions may arise to use the words, or as they are seen in reading, or heard in conversation.

Everything in this book designated as a "Lesson" is to be thoroughly learned. Not a lesson should be omitted, as it has been an object of the author to here present nothing that is useless or unimportant.

This book contains many new features which will commend themselves to progressive teachers. The lessons upon local names will be especially valuable to all North Carolina children, and they should be frequently drilled and exercised in correctly writing the names which appear in the geography and history of the State. We have spent several years in trying to obtain the correct spelling of all principal proper names found in North Carolina, and the orthography as herein set forth is believed to be correct.

The Exercises for Dictation are numerous, and they form a most valuable feature of this book. The exercises are from the writings of prominent North Carolinians, and they are selected with a view both to the interest and instruction of pupils.

There are no diacritical marks used in these lessons, it being the desire of the author to have pupils see and study the words as near as possible in the same form as they will see the words in books and newspapers. Experience has taught us that all arbitrary makings of letters are hinderances instead of helps to a child in *learning* words. As the book is especially to aid Southern children in acquiring the pure language of America as it is found in the South, we have carefully avoided the use of all foreign localism, cockneyisms and affectations in pronunciation and orthography.

To fix in the minds of pupils the words of our language there should be, in addition to the oral spelling, frequent exercises in writing, composition and dictation. While the most important thing is to *learn* the word it is also necessary that pupils know how to *use* the word, and this can be best taught by "using the words."

The lists of words which are classified with respect to their meaning and the common ideas they represent will be found peculiarly helpful to a child, and teachers should use this department of the book as the basis of frequent talks with pupils about the association of ideas as is to be found in words. Pupils should be encouraged to ask the uses of new words when they meet them in their lessons and to investigate the delicate shades of meaning among words which are similar or apparently identical.

THE AMERICAN ALPHABET.

—

ROMAN.

A B C D E F G H I J K L
M N O P Q R S T
U V W X Y Z.

a b c d e f g h i j k l m n
o p q r s t u v w x y z

SCRIPT.

A B C D E F G H I
J K L M N O P
Q R S T U
V W X Y Z

a b c d e f g h i j k l m n
o p q r s t u v w x y z

ROMAN FIGURES.

1 2 3 4 5 6 7 8 9 0

SCRIPT FIGURES.

1 2 3 4 5 6 7 8 9 0

3 1 0

1 4 1

1 6 1 4 1

NORTH CAROLINA
SPELLING-BOOK.

PART I.

LESSON 1.

WORDS OF TWO LETTERS.

am	as	ah	be
am	*as*	*ah*	*be*
an	at	ax	by
an	*at*	*ax*	*by*

LESSON 2

do	go	up	is
do	*go*	*up*	*is*
to	me	on	it
to	*me*	*on*	*it*

It is to go up.   An ax is on it

LESSON 3.

of	he	ox	if
of	*he*	*ox*	*if*
my	in	so	we
my	*in*	*so*	*we*
no	or	us	ye
no	*or*	*us*	*ye*

EXERCISES TO BE WRITTEN.

An ox.
Do we go?
We do go up.

He is by me.
It is an ox.
Is he to go in?

Go up as we go on.

So is he to be by us as we do go in?

LESSON 4.

WORDS OF THREE LETTERS.

cap	had	jib	bob
cap	*had*	*jib*	*bob*
cat	pad	job	bad
cat	*pad*	*job*	*bad*
gab	web	cob	mob
gab	*web*	*cob*	*mob*

LESSON 5.

nob	bib	fob	mad
nob	*bib*	*fob*	*mad*
gad	fib	sob	rub
gad	*fib*	*sob*	*rub*
pup	lap	sop	wed
pup	*lap*	*sop*	*wed*

LESSON 6.

cub	lop	lad	bid
cub	*lop*	*lad*	*bid*
rub	rip	sad	hid
rub	*rip*	*sad*	*hid*
hub	sap	led	did
hub	*sap*	*led*	*did*

LESSON 7.

tub	nip	red	lid
tub	*nip*	*red*	*lid*
rid	sod	log	fog
rid	*sod*	*log*	*fog*
kid	nod	bog	bud
kid	*nod*	*bog*	*bud*

LESSON 8.

mid	rod	bag	cud
mid	*rod*	*bag*	*cud*
wag	odd	dog	mud
wag	*odd*	*dog*	*mud*
hod	pod	hog	sag
hod	*pod*	*hog*	*sag*

LESSON 9.

fag	tag	bug	jug	ham
fag	*tag*	*bug*	*jug*	*ham*
lag	leg	rig	tug	jam
lag	*leg*	*rig*	*tug*	*jam*
rag	keg	wig	mug	ram
rag	*keg*	*wig*	*mug*	*ram*

LESSON 10.

hag	fig	hug	pug	you
hag	*fig*	*hug*	*pug*	*you*
wag	pig	dug	rug	yam
wag	*pig*	*dug*	*rug*	*yam*
top	bed	gem	wen	pet
top	*bed*	*gem*	*wen*	*pet*

LESSON 11.

hat	peg	den	met	rib
hat	*peg*	*den*	*met*	*rib*
pat	fed	men	ten	pin
pat	*fed*	*men*	*ten*	*pin*
rat	hem	let	net	tin
rat	*hem*	*let*	*net*	*tin*

LESSON 12.

mat	hen	pen	yet	lip
mat	*hen*	*pen*	*yet*	*lip*
rip	fix	. sop	mug	cut
rip	*fix*	*sop*	*mug*	*cut*
tip	six	top	gum	nut
tip	*six*	*top*	*gum*	*nut*

LESSON 13.

bit	mix	cot	hum	rut
bit	*mix*	*cot*	*hum*	*rut*
sip	cup	dot	rum	hut
sip	*cup*	*dot*	*rum*	*hut*
pit	hop	got	. gun	jut
pit	*hop*	*got*	*gun*	*jut*
sit	pop	pot	cur	sup
sit	*pop*	*pot*	*cur*	*sup*

LESSON 14.

car	ply	imp	her	for
car	*ply*	*imp*	*her*	*for*
tar	pry	ink	him	his
tar	*pry*	*ink*	*him*	*his*
end	sly	elm	and	gas
end	*sly*	*elm*	*and*	*gas*
arm	oft	elk	ash	get
arm	*oft*	*elk*	*ash*	*get*
fly	egg	ice	asp	cow
fly	*egg*	*ice*	*asp*	*cow*

EXERCISES TO BE WRITTEN.

The dog ran in the lot. Put on the hat and go in the lot to see the pig in the pen. The sun is out and it is hot The rat saw the cat and ran in the box.

LESSON 15.

sky	off	she	nor	gig
men	den	can	our	bye
pur	awl	was	pea	oak
fox	ape	tax	aid	aim
the	you	vat	eye	oar
eat	too	wan	lye	ear
air	war	ant	sea	few
sow	row	new	pew	bee
see	eel	ale	ore	age
ark	inn	own	cow	jaw

LESSON 16.

bay	her	boy	paw	art
day	jay	raw	pay	ace
say	lay	saw	ray	ate
may	out	how	gun	ode
gay	say	key	lie	old
way	coy	bow	nay	fee
toy	joy	low	act	dry
oil	tie	foe	woe	sue
rue	awe	owe	toe	cue

2

EXERCISES TO BE WRITTEN.

I saw the cat run in the box. She did not get the rat, but she saw him run out at the top. The dog was mad, and he bit the man, the pig and the kid. She hid the red cap by the log in the lot. The sun was hid all day by the fog. God is in the sky, we say. The boy had no gun as the bat did fly in the air by him. Do not lie on the bed all day, but get up to see the sun. May did sip the hot tea in the new tin cup. You can not go to see him now. We met six men who got off the car to pay tax.

LESSON 17

WORDS OF FOUR LETTERS.

dice	jade	wide	robe
gage	tide	lobe	race
take	rode	pace	rice
side	lace	nice	wade
face	mice	sage	crop
lice	rage	sake	mace
page	rake	made	vice
make	lade	bade	huge
gaze	mere	lore	lure
bore	nape	cone	bite
sore	cape	pipe	dose

LESSON 18.

mile	pike	game	tale
dole	hale	cake	wile
came	pile	sale	name
like	mole	vile	poke
duke	fame	sell	bile
male	pale	lame	mule
hole	tile	joke	same
dame	pole	bale	wake
core	maze	cure	date
tore	here	kine	cite
haze	gore	lane	bare

LESSON 19.

tame	type	fore	lope	nine
cope	rope	yore	rove	mane
pure	dine	fine	line	mine
pine	wine	vine	bane	pane
sane	cane	wane	base	gate
fate	hate	late	mate	kite
mite	rite	site	dive	cove
zone	hone	tone	vane	vase
case	rate	pate	hive	fume
tune	torn	worn	burn	turn
dray	sail	surf	pond	fish

LESSON 20.

help	yelp	gulp	pulp	damp	camp
lamp	vamp	hemp	gimp	limp	cube
pomp	romp	bump	dump	jump	lump
pump	harp	gasp	hasp	rasp	lisp
wisp	gulf	fact	tact	sect	raft
waft	left	gift	lift	rift	sift
loft	soft	belt	felt	melt	pelt
welt	gilt	hilt	news	tell	bolt
colt	hold	cant	pant	bent	dent
dolt	lent	cent	rent	sent	tent
jolt	vent	went	dint	lint	mint
blue	dime	flag	most	wash	salt

LESSON 21.

int	wept	weep	runt	part	tart
ort	last	mast	zest	kept	cart
lart	mart	cast	fast	past	vast
hart	best	jest	lest	nest	pest
rest	test	vest	west	fire	fist
list	mist	lost	crow	dust	bust
gust	just	must	nest	scab	stab
slab	blab	crab	glib	crib	chub
club	snub	drub	grab	stub	shad
clad	glad	brad	fled	bled	bred

EXERCISES TO BE WRITTEN.

Oh, see what a nice boat sails by the wind on the bay! Four boys and one girl are in the boat, and they seem to have a fine time on the tide. Now the wind dies out, and as the sail does not fill the boat lies still on the bay and the boys must take the oars and row to the land.

LESSON 22.

sped	shed	sled	shod	clod	plod
trod	scud	slug	brag	stag	snag
drag	flag	sham	cram	clam	dram
slam	swam	stem	skim	brim	grim
prim	trim	swim	from	scum	plum
grum	drum	clan	scan	plan	span
bran	glen	chin	skin	spin	grin
twin	chap	flap	slap	snap	trap
chip	ship	skip	chip	slip	down
grip	drip	trip	chop	shop	slop

LESSON 23.

crop	stop	prop	scar	spar	star
stir	blur	slur	spur	flat	plat
spit	spat	fret	whet	slit	grit
shot	blot	clot	plot	spot	trot
shut	smut	glut	flax	bulb	barb
garb	herb	verb	curb	mild	wild
bold	cold	gold	fold	hold	mold
sold	told	band	hand	land	sand
bend	lend	mend	rend	send	tend

The flag of our land is seen on the mast of the ship. It is red, white and blue.

LESSON 24.

bind	find	kind	mind	hind
wind	bond	fond	pond	fund
hard	lard	bird	herd	curd
turf	rich	much	such	itch
feed	heed	need	reed	seed
flee	glee	free	tree	feel
peel	reel	deem	seem	teem
seen	meek	seek	week	beef

LESSON 25.

WORDS OF FIVE LETTERS.

churn	spurn	scalp	clamp
stamp	crimp	chump	clump
crump	sharp	dregs	grasp
lungs	tract	grass	stick
shaft	draft	graft	shift
smelt	spilt	scant	plant
grant	slant	spent	flint
stint	brunt	grunt	swept
snort	blast	chest	write
crept	chart	short	shirt
crest	quest	grist	wrist
burst	mirth	crust	trust
squib	scrub	shrub	shred

LESSON 26.

scrap	strap	strip	scrip	sheen
split	strut	scold	bland	grand
gland	stand	brand	blend	scurf
filch	hatch	lanch	stanch	bunch
hunch	lunch	punch	latch	match
patch	march	harsh	marsh	pouch
torch	lurch	botch	ditch	hitch
pitch	witch	plush	flush	crush
breed	speed	sheen	shine	steel
green	queen	cheek	creek	sheep
creep	steep	cheer	sweep	sheer

EXERCISES TO BE WRITTEN.

Look at the dear babe! How fat are his pink toes! Does it not seem that you can hear him crow as he plays with the toys? How we love this babe, and we hope he will not get sick. We want him to grow up to be a good man. Now he lies down on the mat and plays with the big dog. It is a good dog and he loves the babe.

LESSON 27.

sneer	steer	queer	sleet	fleet
sheet	greet	sweet	brood	geese
goose	bloom	gloom	spoon	swoon
scoop	sloop	droop	loose	swoop
stoop	troop	noose	brook	crook
stood	spool	stool	roost	proof
blood	flood	broom	black	block
snack	crack	track	stack	stock

LESSON 28.

FAMILIAR WORDS OF ONE SYLLABLE.

rook	loom	doom	look	loose	sack
groom	noon	loon	poor	good	neck
boom	moor	took	loop	broom	lick
choose	hook	cook	spoon	swoon	sick
state	wool	coop	room	horse	hock
boon	wood	moon	soon	nook	slack

LESSON 29.

boot	tool	back	rack	lack	tack
root	woof	pack	lock	kick	peck
son	ton	wick	won	roof	tick
pool	deck	hack	smack	pick	nick
yelk	link	hank	silk	lank	mark
bank	mock	sock	milk	sink	ask

LESSON 30.

stuck	hulk	bask	ark	fork	lurk
bulk	rock	risk	lark	cask	mask
earth	luck	mink	dark	task	desk
tank	hasp	wink	hark	dusk	husk
ink	park	pink	jerk	tuft	rusk
elk	dirk	sunk	cork	musk	tusk
gall	spell	gill	pill	will	toll
small	sell	kill	hill	boll	cull

LESSON 31.

dusk	helm	barn	morn	doff	buff
marl	film	yarn	horn	cuff	luff
furl	arm	fern	gaff	muff	puff
hurl	farm	stern	staff	ruff	add
curl	harm	born	tiff	odd	egg
elm	term	corn	post	all	ball
fall	tall	bill	sill	drill	troll
well	stall	ebb	fill	frill	stroll

DICTATION.

You must love your State very much.   It is the best land on earth for a good home.   Do not think that you can find more joy in some State far off, for all who go from our State soon want to come back.   The land here is rich and the crops grow well, the air is fine and pure, and the sun does not get too warm for us, and we will stay at home.

LESSON 32.

call	hall	tell	skill	mill	poll
wall	squall	ill	trill	rill	roll
dull	burr	mass	kiss	fuss	muss
gull	purre	pass	miss	bust	full
hull	bush	grass	loss	mule	hurt
lull	push	guess	moss	baste	mole
inn	bass	less	cross	chaste	lute
bin	lass	bless	cost	haste	waste
light	right	chasm	change	dude	frit

LESSON 33.

fice	slang	grange	jute	craze	fake
flute	blight	tight	prism	. catch	minx
mute	plight	blowze	forge	twixt	text
brute	sight	frounce	grange	nerve	delve
fight	slight	rounce	range	curve	ash
bright	night	trounce	mange	bronze	pose
quack	smirk	shark	flank	drank	clank
brick	check	shirk	spark	stark	stork
shock	crick	speck	town	click	clock

DICTATION.

No one loves a boy or girl who will skulk. It should be our aim to give all the joy we can to our friends. Let us go on the lake in the boat and troll for fish. If we catch some fish we will have them for tea. Our State is a great place for fish, and we ship them to all the large towns.

LESSON 34.

truck	flock	trick	quick	pluck	brink
clink	skulk	frock	stick	drunk	drink
crank	blink	shank	cluck	cloud	flash
trunk	plank	prank	blank	whisk	charm
cliff	brisk	cross	dress	spill	skull
small	sperm	trust	cress	press	guess
swell	stiff	frisk	dross	house	horse
swill	smell	scorn	stove	twirl	skiff
glass	quill	scoff	snarl	stuff	dwell
grass	droll	spell	quaff	still	wren
bliss	class	skill	bluff	chess	tress
gloss	brass	troll	quell	float	bench

LESSON 35.

badge	budge	serge	corse	scorch	rich
edge	judge	verge	clothe	bench	birch
hedge	grudge	dirge	bathe	drench	trench
ledge	hinge	gorge	breathe	quench	iuch
pledge	cringe	urge	sheathe	clinch	flinch
fledge	fringe	surge	wreathe	pinch	gulch
sledge	singe	germ	mouse	batch	hatch
wedge	swinge	corpse	curse	catch	snatch
ridge	twinge	parse	purse	scratch	etch
bridge	lounge	terse	parch	nymph	notch
lodge	plunge	verse	perch	lymph	sylph

LESSON 36.

WORDS OF TWO SYLLABLES, ACCENTED ON THE FIRST.

n' nis	at' las	par' ry	ves' try	pit' y
as sic	suc cor	ber ry	scan ty	tes ty
: is	hon or	fer ry	plen ty	en vy
n cy	ran cor	mer ry	pet ty	ver y
n ny	can dor	sor ry	dit ty	wit ty
p y	splen dor	cur ry	flab by	dol lar
p py	rig or	hur ry	shab by	deal er
p py	vig or	flur ry	lob by	put ty
n dry	val or	en try	lev y	bev y
l fry	fer vor	sen try	prox y	col or

DICTATION.

Knowledge is a golden river—
    From its source true pleasures flow;
Those who would be happy ever
    Should unto its waters go.

Those who sail upon its bosom
    Find more sunbeams in the way
Than if in the gloomy forest
    They had loitered day by day.

Ever rippling gently onward,
    'Neath a bright and cloudless sky,
To the haven it will bear us
    In the joyous "bye and bye."

S. M. S. ROLINSON.

LESSON 37.

WORDS OF TWO SYLLABLES, ACCENTED ON THE FIRST.

la' dy	va' por	pa' cer	gru' el	pu' pil
ti dy	fa vor	ra cer	vi al	pe nal
ho ly	fla vor	gro cer	ve nal	fi nal
li my	sa vor	ci der	o ral	fas ten
sli my	so lo	spi der	chas ten	list en
bo ny	so lar	wo ful	glis ten	soft en
po ny	po lar	po em	oft en	has ten
car ry	sculp tor	dusk y	wor ry	par ty
mar ry	clam or	pal try	ar bor	har boɪ

LESSON 38.

WORDS OF TWO SYLLABLES, ACCENTED ON THE SECOND.

ex ult'	re late'	re main'	sur vey'	de fy'
ex hale	in flate	en gross	de ny	de cry
re spect	col late	dis creet	re boil	a void
a base	trans late	al lay	ex ploit	a droit
de base	re claim	de lay	de coy	en joy
es pouse	pro claim	un say	em ploy	al loy
in case	dis claim	as say	de stroy	an noy
a bate	ex claim	a way	con voy	ex act
de bate	de mean	o bey	ex empt	ex alt
se date	be moan	con vey	ex haust	ex ert
cre ate	re tain	pur vey	ex ile	ex ist

LESSON 39.

WORDS OF TWO SYLLABLES, ACCENTED ON THE FIRST.

noist' en	fe' ver	wa' fer	li' bel	lo' cal
hris ten	o ver	ca per	fo cal	vo cal
o ker	he ro	ti ger	le gal	re gal
i ler	ne gro	ma ker	di al	tri al
a per	tu lip	ta ker	na sal	fa tal
a per	ce dar	ra ker	na tal	ru ral
a per	bri er	ru in	vi tal	o val
i per	fri ar	la bel	to tal	gi ant
a ker	clo ver	lu nar	fo rum	fu el
ha dy	do nor	so ber	du el	cru el

LESSON 40.

WORDS OF TWO SYLLABLES, ACCENTED ON THE SECOND.

e deem'	mis state'	dis may'	sur mount'	re coil'
s teem	re plete	de fray	dis mount	re join
le claim	com plete	ar ray	re count	en join
e lay	se crete	be tray	sub join	dis join
n lay	re cite	por tray	pur loin	en dow
nis lay	in cite	a stray	ca rouse	de vout
lis play	po lite	de spoil	re dound	de vour
e hearse	ig nite	em broil	bap tize	de cay
n camp	un truth	him self	con tent	im part

LESSON 41.

guide	wise	thyme	mound	phrase	use
guile	guise	shrine	bound	muse	fuse
quite	chose	sphere	found	spoil	point
quote	void	pound	hound	broil	coin
hoist	oil	round	close	soil	loin
joist	boil	ground	nose	toil	join
moist	coil	sound	rose	noise	joint
rise	foil	wound	prose	poise	foist

LESSON 42.

WORDS OF TWO SYLLABLES, ACCENTED ON THE FIRST.

lim′ it	ban′ quet	gos′ sip	pop′ lar	ush′ er
sum mit	rus set	bish op	gram mar	nec tar
her mit	riv et	gal lop	pitch er	tar tar
mer it	vel vet	beg gar	butch er	mor tar
spir it	hab it	cel lar	tan gent	rob ber
cul prit	rab bit	pil lar	pun gent	ur gent
vis it	or bit	col lar	frag ment	par rot
pot ash	prof it	dol lar	seg ment	piv ot

DICTATION.

Never misstate an event. It should be the desire of every one to always tell the truth. The boy who has been known to tell an untruth will have a bad name among his playmates, and it will not be easy for him to redeem himself.

LESSON 43.

WORDS OF TWO SYLLABLES, ACCENTED ON THE FIRST.

fig′ ment	can′ dy	al′ ley	chim′ ney	muf′ fler
pig ment	hand y	gal ley	tran sit	gran ger
bal lot	stur dy	val ley	can to	mel on
ram part	stud y	vol ley	shiv er	ser mon
mod est	lack ey	pul ley	sil ver	cou pon
tem pest	jock ey	bar ley	grand son	cov er
for est	mon key	mot ley	sul phur	lack er
ban dy	med ley	don key	mur mur	grot to

LESSON 44.

WORDS OF TWO SYLLABLES, ACCENTED ON THE FIRST.

lamp′ black	fet′ lock	ver′ bal	stat′ ute
bar rack	mat tock	med al	con cave
ran sack	hood wink	ver nal	con clave
ham mock	bul wark	jour nal	oc tave
pad lock	pitch fork	spi nal	res cue
wed lock	dam ask	con trite	val ue
hem lock	sym bol	trib ute	vir tue

DICTATION.

A horseback ride is very pleasant on a bright day. As we gallop along the road through the country we enjoy the fresh and bracing air and the lovely landscape around us. Do you live in the country or do you go there to visit your friends?

3

LESSON 45.

WORDS OF TWO SYLLABLES, ACCENTED ON THE FIRST.

kid' nap	num' ber	in' most	rud' dy	tan' sy
lub ber	bar ber	ut most	gen try	ral ly
blub ber	won der	im post	sul try	sal ly
am ber	yon der	chest nut	hon ey	tal ly
mem ber	gin ger	con test	mon ey	jel ly
lim ber	char ger	mil dew	jour ney	sil ly
tim ber	in quest	ed dy	jer sey	fol ly
cum ber	con quest	gid dy	ker sey	jol ly
lum ber	har vest	mud dy	cler gy	on ly

LESSON 46.

bought	cloud	crown	brown	rout	hour
brought	shroud	frown	clown	couch	trout
fought	ounce	town	gown	slouch	snout
ought	bounce	pouch	flour	mount	pout
caught	flounce	foul	sour	out	spout
wrought	pounce	owl	count	scout	sprout
naught	trout	cowl	fount	gout	choice
fraught	spouse	prowl	fowl	shout	voice
loud	rouse	scowl	howl	our	poise
proud	browse	stout	growl	scour	noise
laid	sea	praise	ease	brief	breach
maid	pea	coarse	tease	grief	preach
board	plea	hoarse	seize	waif	teach

LESSON 47.

WORDS OF THREE SYLLABLES, ACCENTED ON THE FIRST.

leth' ar gy	in' fa my	sal' a ry	fish' er y
bot a ny	en e my	reg is try	crock er y
el e gy	fel o ny	beg gar y	mock er y
prod i gy	col o ny	sor cer y	cook er y
ef fi gy	har mo ny	im age ry	cut ler y
eb o ny	glut ton y	witch er y	gal ler y
en er gy	can o py	butch er y	bur gla ry
lit ur gy	quan ti ty	quack er y	rar i ty

LESSON 48.

hoard	bead	heave	cheese	each	coach
source	mead	weave	raise	beach	roach
course	read	leave	maize	bleach	broach
crease	goad	blue	sheaf	peach	beak
grease	load	flue	leaf	reach	leak
cease	road	glue	loaf	bleak	speak
peace	toad	bye	chief	peak	sneak
lease	aid	lye	lief	creak	freak
blade	bride	place	stage	spike	blame
shade	pride	space	shake	choke	clime
glade	stride	brace	flake	poke	chime
spade	crude	grace	stake	broke	shine
grade	prude	trace	snake	spoke	prime

LESSON 49.

WORDS OF THREE SYLLABLES, ACCENTED ON THE FIRST.

vil' lain y	bat' ter y	chan' cer y	rev' er y
com pa ny	flat ter y	liv er y	nun ner y
lit a ny	lot ter y	cav al ry	ar ter y
lar ce ny	ev er y	rev el ry	mas ter y
des ti ny	gran a ry	mem o ry	fac to ry
cal um ny	gloss a ry	arm o ry	vic to ry
tyr an ny	hus band ry	em er y	his to ry
mys ter y	rob ber y	sym me try	rib ald ry

LESSON 50.

trade	globe	slice	spake	smoke	crime
braid	probe	mice	brake	stroke	plume
jade	gibe	spice	drake	smile	chine
chide	bribe	price	slake	stile	swine
glide	scribe	trice	quake	frame	twine
slide	tribe	twice	strike	shame	twist
shone	snipe	crave	strove	dread	prune
drone	stripe	shave	grove	stead	sweat
prone	tripe	slave	clove	thread	search

DICTATION.

Immortal youth shall crown their deathless fame,
And as their country's glories shall advance
Shall brighter blaze, o'er all the earth, thy name,
Thou first-fought field of Freedom, Alamance.

S. W. WHITING.

LESSON 51.

stone	scope	plate	froze	spread	pearl
scrape	snore	quite	prize	breast	earn
drape	slate	smite	smote	breadth	learn
shape	state	spite	bread	breath	yearn
crape	grate	sprite	dead	earth	meant
grape	grave	drive	head	dearth	health
brine	brave	drove	tread	threat	realm
shown	dear	drear	your	freight	dare
borne	reap	near	hair	treat	wait
shorn	soap	spear	lair	seat	fruit
own	ear	rear	chair	great	suit

LESSON 52.

peal	flail	break	bowl	aim	groan
seal	mail	steak	soul	claim	fain
veal	nail	streak	beam	maim	gain
weal	snail	screak	dream	bean	grain
zeal	pail	squeak	gleam	lean	brain
coal	rail	weak	ream	clean	strain
goal	frail	shriek	cream	glean	lain
shoal	trail	oak	scream	mean	plain
ail	sail	croak	team	wean	slain
bail	tail	soak	steam	mien	main
fail	vail	deal	foam	moan	pain
hail	quail	heal	loam	loan	rain
jail	wail	meal	roam	roan	train

LESSON 53.

WORDS OF TWO SYLLABLES, ACCENTED ON THE FIRST.

buck' et	mal' let	brack' et	mul' let	car' pet
blank et	pal let	tick et	ham let	clar et
mar ket	wal let	crick et	gim let	gar ret
bas ket	buf fet	wick et	in let	fer ret
cas ket	fidg et	dock et	bon net	tur ret
bris ket	budg et	pock et	son net	off set
mus ket	rack et	sock et	gar ment	on set
tab let	latch et	bil let	cor net	cor set
trip let	fresh et	fil let	hor net	bul let
gob let	jack et	mil let	trum pet	dul cet

LESSON 54.

WORDS OF THREE SYLLABLES, ACCENTED ON THE FIRST.

pol' y glot	run' a way	mer' ri ment	sol' ven cy
ber ga mot	car a way	det ri ment	sum ma ry
an te past	ban ish ment	sen ti ment	land la dy
in ter est	blan dish ment	doc u ment	rem e dy
pen te cost	pun ish ment	teg u ment	com e dy
hal i but	rav ish ment	mon u ment	per fi dy
fur be low	ped i ment	ten den cy	mel o dy
cic a trix	sed i ment	pun gen cy	mon o dy
par a dox	al i ment	clem en cy	par o dy
sar do nyx	com pli ment	cur ren cy	pros o dy
hol i day	lin i ment	bank rupt cy	cus to dy

LESSON 55.

blown	fear	sear	tour	moat
flown	year	tear	eaves	oar
sown	hear	wear	leaves	roar
grown	shear	swear	stilts	soar

EXERCISES FOR DICTATION.

Wanted: Men.
Not *systems* fit and wise,
Not *faiths* with *rigid* eyes,
Not *wealth* in *mountain* piles,
Not *power* with *gracious* smiles,
Not even the *potent* pen,
   Wanted: Men.

Wanted: Deeds.
Not words of *winning* note,
Not *thoughts* from life *remote*,
Not fond *religious* airs,
Not sweetly *languid prayers*,
Not love of *scented* creeds,
   Wanted: Deeds.

Men and Deeds,—
Men that can dare and do,
Not *longings* for the new,
Not *pratings* for the old,
Good life and *action* bold,
These the *occasion* needs;
   Men and Deeds.   *—Selected.*

LESSON 56.

pair	neat	guilt	dew	view	blow
stair	oat	court	few	pew	flow
heir	bloat	saint	hew	crew	glow
greaves	coat	east	chew	screw	slow
pains	goat	beast	view	drew	mow
shears	float	least	blew	grew	row
guess	weight	feast	clew	shrew	snow
guest	bait	yeast	flew	strew	crow
feat	gait	boast	brew	stew	grow
heat	plait	roast	slew	strow	bow
bleat	trait	toast	mew	show	sow
meat	built	waist	new	low	stow
lane	cheap	clear	air	eat	tier

LESSON 57.

WORDS OF THREE SYLLABLES, ACCENTED ON THE FIRST.

ob′ lo quy	am′ i ty	up′ per most	roy′ al ty
sin ew y	jol li ty	min is try	u su ry
gal ax y	nul li ty	in dus try	ra pi er
ped ant ry	en mi ty	cent u ry	nau ti lus
in fant ry	san i ty	mer cu ry	pau ci ty
gal lant ry	van i ty	ty po graph	man i fest
big ot ry	bal co ny	an gli can	treach er y
an ces try	len i ty	dy nas ty	ed u cate
tap es try	dig ni ty	gay e ty	cav al ry
trin i ty	dep u ty	loy al ty	cal va ry

LESSON 58.

WORDS OF TWO SYLLABLES, ACCENTED ON THE FIRST.

ar' lor	bur' nish	mess' mate	state' ment	heav' en
ar ner	pun ish	re search	rai ment	leav en
rt ful	clown ish	room mate	leath ern	heav y
lan dish	snap pish	clean ly	pleas ant	read y
ran dish	par ish	typ ist	pleas ure	health y
ub bish	cher ish	stag nate	meas ure	wealth y
elf ish	flour ish	fil trate	treas ure	feath er
hurl ish	nour ish	pros trate	threat en	leath er

LESSON 59.

WORDS OF TWO SYLLABLES, ACCENTED ON THE SECOND.

e get'	re act'	ja pan'	e lect'	con duct'
or get	en act	tre pan	se lect	ob struct
e gret	com pact	rat tan	re flect	in struct
e set	re fract	di van	in flect	con struct
in fit	com pel	be gin	neg lect	re plant
ub mit	dis pel	with in	col lect	im plant
d mit	ex pel	pro ject	con nect	sup plant
mit	re pel	tra ject	re spect	dis plant
e mit	im pel	ob ject	sus pect	trans plant
rans mit	pro pel	sub ject	e rect	de scent
om mit	fore tell	de ject	ex tinct	la ment
er mit	ful fill	de fect	de funct	aug ment
e fit	dis till	af fect	de coct	af fix
ic quit	in still	ef fect	de duct	de bar

LESSON 60.

WORDS OF TWO SYLLABLES, ACCENTED ON THE FIRST.

crank′ y	teth′ er	el′ der	doc′ tor	tan′ ner
car ly	sis ter	nev er	tin der	in ner
ear nest	fos ter	ev er	ped dler	din ner
ban ter	bat ter	sev er	til ler	tin ner
can ter	hat ter	liv er	sut ler	sin ner
cen ter	mat ter	riv er	ham mer	cor ner
en ter	tat ter	man or	ram mer	tam per
win ter	let ter	ten or	sum mer	tem per
fes ter	fet ter	vic tor	ban ner	sim per

EXERCISES FOR DICTATION.

The first great maxim of human conduct, that which it is all-important to impress on the understandings of young men, and recommend to their hearty adoption, is—above all things, in all circumstances, and under every emergency—to preserve a clean heart and an honest purpose.

Integrity, firm, determined integrity, is that quality which, of all others, raises man to the highest dignity of his nature, and fits him to adorn and bless the sphere in which he is appointed to move. Without it, neither genius nor learning, neither the gifts of God nor human exertions, can avail aught for the accomplishment of the great objects of human existence.

Integrity is the crowning virtue—integrity is the pervading principle which ought to regulate, guide, control and vivify every impulse, desire and action.—WILLIAM GASTON.

LESSON 61.

WORDS OF TWO SYLLABLES, ACCENTED ON THE FIRST.

tun' nel	grav' el	up' per	hov' el	len' til
fun nel	bev el	sup per	nov el	cav il
ker nel	lev el	ves per	mar vel	civ il
gos pel	rev el	reb el	pen cil	an vil
bar rel	clap per	can cel	sin ful	cor al
sor rel	pep per	cam el	aw ful	bar ter
mor sel	dip per	pan el	per il	mas ter
ves sel	cop per	ken nel	ton sil	cas tor
tin sel	hop per	fen nel	fos sil	pas tor

LESSON 62.

WORDS OF FOUR SYLALBLES, ACCENTED ON THE FIRST.

pres' by ter y	sal' u ta ry	dil' a to ry
prom is so ry	cap il la ry	or a to ry
pred a to ry	cor ol la ry	dor mi to ry
pref a to ry	ad ver sa ry	mon i to ry
pul sa to ry	al a bas ter	ter ri to ry
aud it o ry	plan et a ry	tran si to ry
ex cre to ry	stat u a ry	in ven to ry
mon as ter y	sanct u a ry	con tro ver sy
al le go ry	sumpt u a ry	leg is la tive
des ul to ry	man da to ry	leg is la ture
trib u ta ry	pur ga to ry	leg is la tor

LESSON 63.

wealth	grant	sauce	gawk	drawl	yawl
stealth	slant	cause	hawk	fawn	dawn
cleanse	large	gauze	haul	lawn	yawn
dreamt	charge	clause	maul	pawn	dwarf
daunt	barge	pause	awl	spawn	watch
haunt	salve	squash	bawl	brawn	vault
flaunt	scarf	wash	sprawl	drawn	fault
taunt	fraud	swash	brawl	naught	aught
vaunt	broad	quash	crawl	caught	taugh
mourn	leap	smear	fair	beat	bier
stain	heap	blear	tear	chintz	pier

LESSON 64.

WORDS OF TWO SYLLABLES, ACCENTED ON THE FIRST.

cor′ ban	in′ gress	con′ gress	ab′ ject
kitch en	mus lin	prog ress	ob ject
chick en	res in	for tress	sub ject
mar tin	ros in	mis tress	ver dict
slov en	mat in	but tress	rel ict
ur chin	sat in	rick ets	dis trict
dol phin	spav in	spir its	in stinc
pip pin	wel kin	mys tic	pre cinc
har ness	ten don	brick bat	gib bet
wit ness	cor don	per fect	lan cet

LESSON 65.

WORDS OF FOUR SYLLABLES, THE PRIMARY ACCENT ON
THE FIRST.

it' o miz er	ex' cel len cy	sec' ond a ry	mil' li ner y
in gli can ism	com pe ten cy	ex em pla ry	or di na ry
u mi na ry	im po ten cy	an ti qua ry	sem i na ry
u li na ry	mis cel la ny	tit u la ry	lit er a ry
no ment a ry	nec es sa ry	cus tom a ry	ar bi tra ry
ore vi a ry	ig no min y	hon or a ry	em is sa ry
f fi ca cy	cer e mo ny	mer ce na ry	cem e ter y
lel i ca cy	al i mo ny	pul mo na ry	sec re ta ry
n tri' ca cy	mat ri mo ny	sub lu na ry	mil i ta ry
ob sti na cy	pat ri mo ny	form u la ry	sol i ta ry
ic cu ra cy	par si mo ny	ad ver sa ry	sed en ta ry
x i gen cy	tes ti mo ny	com mis sa ry	vol un ta ry

DICTATION.

Let our ambition be not mainly the attainment of honor,
wealth or influence, for they are disappointing; but let it be
duty well done. *That* is true ambition. Let North Caro-
inians love their native State. Let them appreciate her noble
sons and daughters, her forests and streams, her mountains
and valleys, her history and her gallant defense of human
rights. When we contend for preferment among our fellow-
men, let it be that noble contention which aims at bettering
the condition of our State and country. Let our ambition be
ever so great if it is guided by a due sense of duty to God,
our neighbor, and our native land.—SIDNEY M. FINGER.

LESSON 66.

WORDS OF TWO SYLLABLES, ACCENTED ON THE FIRST.

va' cant	o' vert	si' lent	va' ry	ha' zy
flu ent	ru by	case ment	du ty	la zy
fre quent	spi cy	pave ment	na vy	slea zy
se quent	tri dent	move ment	gra vy	bar gain
ri ot	pru dent	mo ment	safe ty	cap tain
pi lot	stu dent	ci pher	sure ty	cer tain
bare foot	a gent	need y	glo ry	vil lain
pre cept	re gent	cro ny	sto ry	vi sor
post script	co gent	pu ny	cra zy	slan der
var nish	in mate	tri umph	health ful	prel ate

LESSON 67.

WORDS OF THREE SYLLABLES, ACCENTED ON THE FIRST.

hec' to graph	pa' pa cy	pri' va cy	o' ri ent
sten o graph	re gen cy	po ten cy	a pri cot
chro no graph	pi ra cy	pli an cy	va can cy
in stru ment	co gen cy	flu en cy	ob lo quy
con ti nent	se cre cy	mu ti ny	di a ry
id i ot	leg a cy	scru ti ny	ro sa ry
char i ot	fal la cy	i ron y	no ta ry
va gran cy	pol i cy	cus to dy	gro cer y
lu na cy	in fan cy	cru ci fix	dra per y
de cen cy	con stan cy	di a lect	i vo ry

LESSON 68.

WORDS OF TWO SYLLABLES, ACCENTED ON THE FIRST.

ur' nish	skit' tish	vi' brate	break' fast	tread' le
)lem ish	lav ish	pi rate	stead fast	jeal ous
kir mish	rav ish	cu rate	mead ow	zeal ous
'an ish	pub lish	pri vate	frus trate	zeal ot
in ish	sen ate	fi nite	dic tate	stealth y
;ar nish	in grate	post age	tes tate	stead y
ar nish	pal ate	plu mage	pleas ant	cli mate
u tor	qui et	tu mor	ba sis	ty rant
)ri or	se cret	la bor	u nit	de cent
'a zor	po et	o dor	cri sis	re cent
u ror	di et	gra ver	cru et	va grant

LESSON 69.

WORDS OF THREE SYLLABLES, ACCENTED ON THE FIRST.

n' ju ry	po' e sy	nov' el ty	con' tra ry
)er ju ry	cru el ty	fac ul ty	ut ter most
)en u ry	pu ri ty	mod es ty	cel e ry
ux u ry	den si ty	am nes ty	ple na ry
1er e sy	en ti ty	bot a ny	sa li ent
:m bas sy	cav i ty	boun te ous	le ni ent
le i ty	lev i ty	mount ain ous	ve he ment
'e al ty	lax i ty	coun ter feit	bri er y
)i e ty	pen al ty	fraud u lent	wa ter y

LESSON 70.

WORDS OF THREE SYLLABLES, ACCENTED ON THE SECOND.

ex am' ine	pur vey' or	ex cite' ment
ex am ple	sur vey or	ap pen dix
ex hib it	sur vey ing	au tum nal
ex ot ic	en deav or	how ev er
ex ist ence	dis burse ment	em bar rass
a base ment	in dorse ment	in stall ment
al lure ment	arch bish op	in thrall ment
de base ment	ad vent ure	hy drau lics
in cite ment	dis fran chise	en joy ment
en slave ment	de pos it	em ploy ment
a maze ment	re pos it	em bar go
in qui ry	at trib ute	im prove ment
un ea sy	im mod est	at tor ney
con vey ance	un luck y	an noy ance

DICTATION.

State pride is an active desire to see our immediate country prosperous and happy. It has its origin in that love for the land of our birth, which is one of the strongest instincts of our nature, and incites nobler actions and induces greater sacrifices than any other impulse of man's bosom. Love of birthplace and home is developed simultaneously with those warm affections for parents, brothers, friends, that exist around the family hearth, and which, if cultivated, cluster ever after about the human heart.—W. W. AVERY.

LESSON 71.

WORDS OF THREE SYLLABLES, ACCENTED ON THE SECOND.

in fer' nal	in clem' ent	ap par' el	as sev' er
ma ter nal	de ter mine	u ten sil	dis sev er
pa ter nal	as sas sin	un civ il	de liv er
e ter nal	im mor tal	tri umph al	e lix ir
in ter nal	pa rent al	in form al	pre cep tor
di ur nal	ac quit tal	bap tis mal	com pos ite
noc tur nal	en am el	a ban don	en am or
un cer tain	im pan el	pi las ter	to bac co

LESSON 72.

WORDS OF TWO SYLLABLES, ACCENTED ON THE FIRST.

clap' per	pon' der	ter' ror	scof' fer	mam' mon
skip per	un der	mir ror	prof fer	gam mon
slip per	blun der	hor ror	proc tor	com mon
crop per	plun der	cen sor	chan nel	gal lon
pros per	thun der	spon sor	cud gel	lem on
less er	sun der	satch el	hatch et	can non
dress er	or der	flan nel	trav el	cit ron
af ter	bor der	chap el	pom mel	ten on
raft er	mur der	grav el	bush el	pis ton
rant er	dif fer	of fer	chan cel	sex ton
hin der	er ror	cof fer	fel on	stuc co

4

LESSON 73.

WORDS OF TWO SYLLABLES, ACCENTED ON THE FIRST.

dri' ver	trem' or	pain' ful	co' lon	gra' ter
ma jor	hu mor	spoon ful	de mon	fo cus
mi nor	ru mor	tune ful	i ron	mu cus
stu por	con jure	hope ful	a pron	fla gran
vi tal	per jure	care ful	sales man	rep tile
e qual	pleas ure	frac ture	states man	fer tile
sur feit	meas ure	cul ture	free dom	hos tile
an gel	treas ure	fix ture	luke warm	flex tile
an cient	cen sure	cam phor	tri form	verd ur
wea sel	press ure	prom ise	mor tise	fig ure

LESSON 74.

WORDS OF TWO SYLLABLES, ACCENTED ON THE FIRST.

jew' el	fis' sure	tur' key	prac' tice	in' jure
new el	ire ful	eye let	trav erse	fac ile
fer ule	dire ful	tu mult	ad verse	serv ile
tre foil	use ful	bol ster	pack horse	dac tyl
neu tral	grate ful	hol ster	ref use	duc tile
plu ral	spite ful	oak um	man date	leg ate
por tal	waste ful	quo rum	ag ate	in grate
bru tal	faith ful	stra tum	mis sile	phys ic
brace let	youth ful	fore man	doc ile	sub tile
out wit	pru dent	in fect	in duct	ex tol

LESSON 75.

WORDS OF TWO SYLLABLES, ACCENTED ON THE FIRST.

watch′ fire	bal′ last	bow′ line	mon′ grel
wash out	con cert	mid way	nick el
wash house	ef fort	es say	nerv ine
ware room	pur port	com fort	dead line
zig zag	tran script	cov ert	dai ly
unc tion	con script	bom bast	dis count
ul ster	bank rupt	court ship	drum ming
tin type	eld est	flim sy	dol man
sun burn	neph ew	clum sy	eu chre
shrink age	sin ew	swel try	teach er

DICTATION.

The composition of man is threefold: physical, intellectual, and moral. It is the justly proportioned composition of these three that constitutes the real excellence of perfect manhood— that creature, made a little lower than the angels, the noblest image of God.

Perhaps no character in history can be pronounced truly great without this combination; certainly not if the moral attributes be deficient.—Z. B. VANCE.

"Carolina! Carolina! Heaven's blessings attend her!
While we live we will cherish, protect and defend her;
Though the scorner may sneer at and witlings defame her,
Our hearts swell with gladness whenever we name her."

LESSON 76.

WORDS OF TWO SYLLABLES, ACCENTED ON THE FIRST.

re′ flex	in′ dex	driz′ zly	bro′ ker
sher bet	syn tax	ver y	back wood
pro rate	com plex	gris ly	bum mer
pret zel	vor tex	guilt y	ca ble
pan nier	con vex	fren zy	chlo ral
func tion	af flux	gyp sy	chro mo
ger man	con flux	drop sy	cob web
hag gle	ef flux	scrub by	rack et
hym nal	in flux	light wood	eye glass
ku klux	con text	mes sage	boy cot

LESSON 77.

WORDS OF TWO SYLLABLES, ACCENTED ON THE SECOND.

ap plause′	suf fuse′	com prise′	re treat′	ad here
ap pease	in fuse	chas tise	un loose	en dear
re pose	con fuse	ad vise	de bauch	re hear
pro pose	a muse	de vise	re call	u surp
im pose	re cruit	re vise	be fall	ap pear
com pose	de feat	dis guise	with al	tat too
trans pose	dis please	fore close	fore stall	en trap
a buse	dis ease	in close	fore warn	in wrap
ac cuse	pre mise	dis close	de fault	un ship
ex cuse	sur mise	es cheat	as sault	e quip
re fuse	de spise	re peat	with draw	en camp
dif fuse	a rise	en treat	a sleep	de camp

LESSON 78.

WORDS OF TWO SYLLABLES, ACCENTED ON THE FIRST.

sports' man	mind' ful	watch' ful	nose' gay	el' bow
mon ster	peace ful	frail ty	mead ow	bor row
mile stone	hate ful	dain ty	min now	fel low
hail stone	wake ful	cam bric	mar row	fol low
hy phen	guile ful	shoul der	har row	cal lus
war fare	dole ful	dai ry	spar row	shad ow
as ure	shame ful	dai ly	yar row	hal low
seiz ure	mourn ful	dai sy	yel low	bil low
rea tise	fear ful	ea sy	tal low	hol low
ike wise	cheer ful	trea ty	fal low	ar row
loor case	right ful	hear say	win dow	far row
tair case	fruit ful	drear y	win now	nar row

LESSON 79.

WORDS OF TWO SYLLABLES, ACCENTED ON THE SECOND.

re solve'	de serve'	as perse'	con form'	re turn'
dis solve	con dense	dis perse	per form	a verse
e volve	im mense	re mark	con fer	re verse
re volve	de fense	un mask	trans fer	in verse
e volve	of fense	fare well	con cern	in dorse
a bode	dis pense	un furl	dis cern	re morse
un nerve	pre tense	de form	a dorn	dis burse
ob serve	col lapse	re form	for lorn	di verge
sub serve	im merse	in form	ad journ	for give

LESSON 80.

THE SOUND OF *a* IN *all* (=*aw*) AND IN *what* (=*o*).

squan der	law suit	taw ny	slaugh ter	scal lop
plaud it	wa ter	taw dry	al ter	wan der
brawn y	daugh ter	fault y	fal ter	draw er
quar ry	au thor	pau per	quar ter	wal nut
flaw y	sau cy	squad ron	law yer	pal try
saw pit	gaud y	sau cer	saw yer	al most
with al	de bauch	haught y	hal ter	au tumn
be fall	as sault	law less	laun dry	out law
re call	fore warn	ap plause	war rior	de fault
fore stall	what not	aw ful	far 'ther	au burn

DICTATION.

The name of the City of Raleigh awakens a long train of far-reaching associations. It summons from the placid deeps of the past the memory of a grand and gallant hero, the towering shade and central figure of England's golden Elizabethian age; it evokes, in quiet majesty, the form of SIR WALTER RALEIGH, the statesman and soldier, the sailor and courtier, the poet and philosopher, the chemist and historian, and the martyr in the cause of human freedom. On him, it was once said, the old world gazed as a star! while from the new, where crystal cliffs of Mt. Raleigh, amid the solitudes of arctic seas, shimmer beneath the aurora's rays, the reflection of his fame flashed back! flashed over old ocean's wrinkled wastes three centuries ago, when the keels of his intrepid fleet first cleft the inland waters of the hemisphere which we now inhabit.—JOSEPH W. HOLDEN.

LESSON 81.

WORDS OF TWO SYLLABLES, ACCENTED ON THE FIRST.

bri' dal	boast' ful	wear' y	wil' low	mal' low
oat meal	scant ling	que ry	mel low	pil low
spi ral	peo ple	off ing	mor row	shal low
flo ral	thrall dom	stuff ing	sor row	fur row
wee vil	watch man	bri ny	bur row	wid ow
twink ling	cap tive	con stant	mas sive	pas sion
shil ling	fur long	ex tant	pas sive	ac tion
sap ling	os trich	sex tant	stat ue	pen sion
strip ling	gal lant	ac cent	stat ute	ces sion
dump ling	dor mant	ad vent	mo tion	ten sion
dar ling	ten ant	cres cent	no tion	ver sion

LESSON 82.

WORDS OF TWO SYLLABLES, ACCENTED ON THE SECOND.

ab solve'	dis patch'	in ter'	de fer'	a dopt'
re serve	re fresh	ab hor	re fer	ab rupt
pre serve	de bark	oc cur	pre fer	cor rupt
con serve	em bark	in cur	in fer	a part
at tach	trans form	con cur	sham poo	de part
de tach	con demn	re cur	cra vat	im part
en rich	con tempt	de mur	co quet	a mong
re trench	con verse	a las	be set	be long
in trench	per verse	a mend	at tempt	a long

LESSON 83.

WORDS OF TWO SYLLABLES, ACCENTED ON THE FIRST.

sprink′ ling	fes′ tive	in′ stant	ar′ dent	fac′ tion
star ling	rem nant	ser aph	lo tion	ses sion
ster ling	pen nant	na tive	por tion	dic tion
stock ing	flip pant	plain tive	na tion	fic tion
mid dling	quad rant	mo tive	ra tion	suc tion
gos ling	ar rant	sport ive	sta tion	mis sion
scant ling	war rant	hire ling	man sion	cap tion
her ring	parch ment	year ling	frac tion	op tion
ob long	pleas ant	tri umph	trac tion .	flec tion
head long	peas ant	tri glyph	men tion	auc tion
mis sive	dis tant	tru ant	junc tion	cau tion

LESSON 84.

WORDS OF TWO SYLLABLES, ACCENTED ON THE SECOND.

ca jole′	ca nine′	sus tain′	tri une′	re vere′
con sole	re pine	do main	com mune	se vere
mis rule	su pine	re frain	es cape	com peer
hu mane	en shrine	re strain	e lope	ca reer
in sane	en twine	dis train	de clare	bre vier
ob scene	be tween	con strain	in snare	bab oon
gan grene	ca reen	con tain	de spair	buf foon
con vene	cam paign	ob tain	pre pare	dra goon
com bine	ar raign	de tain	re pair	rac coon
de fine	or dain	per tain	com pare	doub loon
re fine	dis dain	at tain	im pair	bal loon

LESSON 85.

WORDS OF TWO SYLLABLES, ACCENTED ON THE SECOND.

per spire′	con spire′	im mure′	com mute′	re bate′
con fine	re gain	post pone	sin cere	pla toon
sa line	com plain	de throne	ad here	har poon
de cline	ex plain	en throne	co here	fes toon
di vine	ab stain	a tone	aus tere	dis own
ex pire	a dore	in ure	per mute	un true
de sire	be fore	im pure	com pute	im peach
re tire	de plore	as sure	de pute	ap proach
en tire	im plore	ma ture	dis pute	en croach
at tire	ex plore	de cease	re ceive	re proach
re quire	re store	de crease	per ceive	be seech
in quire	se cure	re lease	de rive	con geal
es quire	pro cure	pro mote	de prive	re peal
ac quire	ob scure	de note	ar rive	ap peal
as pire	en dure	re fute	con trive	re veal

DICTATION.

Tell me, ye winds, if e'er ye rest
Your wings on fairer land,
Save when near Araby the blest
Ye scent its fragrant strand?
Tell me, ye Spirits of the Air,
Know ye a region anywhere,
By night or day that can compare
With Carolina, bright and fair?

JAMES A. DELKE.

LESSON 86.

WORDS OF TWO SYLLABLES, ACCENTED ON THE FIRST.

neu' ter	out' ward	man' ger	ti' dings	treat' ment
pew ter	wa ges	stran ger	moor ings	ran kle
bea ver	cray on	dan ger	twee zers	neck tie
cleav er	a corn	ci pher	heed less	head light
weav er	home spun	twi light	e gress	halt er
sew er	snow drop	moon light	re gress	wain scot
lay er	fore top	day light	cy press	main mast
may or	main top	sky light	fa mous	hind most
col ter	shoul der	fore sight	vi nous	fore most
trai tor	mold er	por trait	po rous	by law
home ward	ran ger	bow sprit	griev ous	rain bow

LESSON 87.

WORDS OF TWO SYLLABLES, ACCENTED ON THE SECOND.

in crease'	re mote'	re prieve'	dis seize'	cur tail'
re spire	ad jure	sa lute	re vive	gen teel
trans pire	al lure	di lute	sur vive	as sail
in spire	de mure	pol lute	al lude	en tail
pre cise	be have	a light	ap prise	de tail
con cise	en slave	de light	as size	re tail
mo rose	for gave	a right	re lief	a vail
jo cose	en grave	af fright	be hoof	pre vail
im brue	de prave	re move	a loof	be wail
dis course	sub due	be hoove	re proof	con trol
u nite	ac crue	ap prove	ob lige	en roll

LESSON 88.

WORDS OF TWO SYLLABLES, ACCENTED ON THE FIRST.

mor' al	dam' sel	gam' ble	cus' tom	pen' man
cen tral	ten dril	mad am	bot tom	peev ish
vas sal	ster ile	bed lam	plat form	work man
den tal	nos tril	bal sam	sar casm	kins man
men tal	tran quil	em blem	mi asm	hunts man
mor tal	gam bol	prob lem	fan tasm	foot man
ves tal	sym bol	sys tem	soph ism	cap stan
fis cal	pis tol	pil grim	bap tism	sil van
form al	hand ful	king dom	al um	fam ine
dis mal	wish ful	sel dom	vel lum	en gine
rev el	bash ful	wis dom	min im	er mine

. LESSON 89.

WORDS OF THREE SYLLABLES, ACCENTED ON THE SECOND.

sur ren' der	dis cred' it	en vel' op	in clo' sure
dis or der	de crep it	de vel op	dis clo sure
en gen der	in her it	en cum ber	com po sure
me an der	de mer it	con sid er	ex po sure
nar cis sus	pome gran ate	be wil der	fore clo sure
co los sus	ex am ple	mis for tune	dis cov er
im per fect	in tes tate	a pos tate	dis col or
in ter pret	me men to	pro mul gate	re cov er
in hab it	mu lat to	in car nate	dis com fit
pro hib it	pal met to	vol ca no	dis as ter

LESSON 90.

WORDS OF TWO SYLLABLES, ACCENTED ON THE FIRST.

tim' brel	skill' ful	min' ion	nos' trum	ver' min
mon grel	help ful	ven om	frus trum	doc trine
quar rel	bliss ful	tran som	tur ban	des tine
squir rel	fret ful	blos som	or gan	phal anx
min strel	hurt ful	phan tom	or phan	si ren

DICTATION.

Education not merely discloses and develops the beauty of the mind, but it is an essential instrument of usefulness and power. This particular aspect of education is perhaps best illustrated in the common school system, in which the design is, first, to lay the solid foundation of all future attainments and elegant ornaments.

In education, the same principles should hold as in domestic economy. A man of sense will first lay in a sufficiency of articles strictly necessary to the use and comfort of the family. He may then, if his means permit, and to the extent that they permit, indulge his taste for the merely elegant and ornamental· So in education.

The young man should be so thoroughly grounded in the elements of practical knowledge as to qualify him to gain a respectable living by the industrious use of his time and talents. He may then, very properly, seek to have such an acquaintance with literature, science, and art as shall render him not only a strong, but a shining, character, always bearing in mind the maxim, "'Tis only solid bodies polish well."—JOSEPH M. ATKINSON.

LESSON 91.

WORDS OF TWO SYLLABLES, ACCENTED ON THE FIRST, *ain* IS SOUNDED AS *in*.

liq' uid	sun' burnt	pres' ent	big' ot	jeal' ous
liq uor	ab bot	ad vent	fag got	pomp ous
piq uant	vil lain	man ners	spig ot	won drous
an nals	plant ain	nip pers	cur rent	lep rous
mit tens	cur tain	scis sors	ab sent	mon strous
sum mons	dol phin	car cass	con vent	nerv ous
for ceps	tress es	cut lass	fer ment	tor ment
pinch ers	trap pings	com pass	in got	vest ment
snuf fers	ser pent	mat tress	end less	zeal ot
solv ent	tor rent	ab scess	zeal ous	tap root

LESSON 92.

IN THE FOLLOWING WORDS *tu* IS LIKE *ch*.

mois' ture	rap' ture	fu' ture	stric' ture
na ture	scrip ture	join ture	struc ture
nur ture	cap ture	junc ture	fu ture
or dure	cinc ture	lec ture	tex ture
pas ture	crea ture	mix ture	tinc ture
pic ture	cul ture	sculp ture	tor ture
pos ture	fea ture	stat ure	ven ture
punc ture	frac ture	ges ture	ver dure

LESSON 93.

WORDS OF TWO SYLLABLES, ACCENTED ON THE SECOND.

ad dress'	ex cess'	dis trust'	im port'	ar rest'
ca ress	con fess	mis trust	com port	de test
re dress	un less	un mixt	sup port	con test
ag gress	dis tress	a vert	trans port	pro test
trans gress	as sess	sub vert	re sort	at test
de press	pos sess	re vert	as sort	di vest
re press	a miss	di vert	re tort	in vest
im press	re miss	con vert	con tort	be quest
op press	dis miss	per vert	dis tort	re quest
sup press	em boss	a lert	ex tort	sub sist
ex press	a cross	in ert	un hurt	de sist

LESSON 94.

WORDS OF TWO SYLLABLES, ACCENTED ON THE SECOND.

tra peze'	ca det'	pro tect'	dis sent'	ap point'
a mass	dis cuss	ex pert	con trast	in sist
re pass	re cast	de sert	a midst	re sist
sur pass	ex haust	in sert	in fest	con sist
cui rass	ro bust	as sert	sug gest	per sist
mo rass	ad just	es cort	di gest	as sist
ac cess	un just	de port	be hest	un twist
re cess	en trust	re port	mo lest	re coil
ca vort	in fract	ad dict	in tent	dis joint
cam paign	sub tract	pre dict	con tent	a noint
coy ote	de tract	af flict	ex tent	ac count

LESSON 95.

WORDS OF TWO SYLLABLES, ACCENTED ON THE FIRST.

shel' ter	tum' bler	shud' der	lob' ster	tor' por
fil ter	sad dler	rud der	chat ter	bar ren
mil ler	ant ler	can non	shat ter	rob in
chap ter	skim mer	gan der	clut ter	cof fin
suf fer	glim mer	pan der	flut ter	muf fin
pil fer	prop er	gen der	plat ter	bod kin
badg er	lad der	slen der	smat ter	wel kin
ledg er	mad der	ren der	spat ter	nap kin
bank er	fod der	ten der	shiv er	gob lin
cank er	ul cer	cin der	sliv er	mus lin
hank er	char ter	lit ter	quiv er	lu cid
can cer	glis ter	mon ster	cul ver	bar on

DICTATION.

"Knowledge is power," and the printing-press has brought knowledge within the reach of all. The result has been an uplifting of the human race such as could not have been attained by any other means. The clicking of the bits of metal in the printer's hand is a music that is daily heard around the world and that will last as long as the centuries. The white sheets passed through the presses of the publisher are wings on which the burning words, the ideas fresh from the mental alchemy of those in the forefront of the battle of life, are borne to the ends of the earth.—JAMES IREDELL MCREE.

LESSON 96.

WORDS OF TWO SYLLABLES, ACCENTED ON THE SECOND.

mis print'	re tract'	in flict'	e vent'	al low'
ex cise	con tract	con flict	re print	en dow
o zone	pro tract	de pict	pre text	be dew
here in	ab stract	re strict	re lax	re new
per haps	dis tract	suc cinct	per plex	fore tell
re volt	ex tract	dis tinct	an nex	be low
a dult	trans act	pre fix	de vour	be stow
re sult	re ject	trans fix	a loud	af front
in sult	e ject	pro lix	com plaint	con front
con sult	in ject	ce ment	re straint	re prove
de cant	cor rect	con sent	con straint	dis prove
re cant	di rect	fo ment	dis traint	im prove
a bet	de tect	fer ment	ac quaint	re ply

LESSON 97.

WORDS OF THREE SYLLABLES, ACCENTED ON THE FIRST.

por' ti co	in' ter im	cred' it or	droll' er y
au di tor	cham ber lain	ed it or	qual i ty
al ma nac	di a phragm	coun sel or	lau re ate
wa ter fall	re qui em	or a tor	buoy an cy
quad ra ture	pol i tics	sen a tor	dent ist ry
cov ert ure	cop per as	pow er ful	soph ist ry
e qui nox	an ces tor	bay o net	proph e cy
coun ter sign	mon i tor	fruit er y	por phy ry

LESSON 98.

WORDS OF TWO SYLLABLES, ACCENTED ON THE FIRST.

sur′ feit	for′ ward	fort′ une	pea′ nut	in′ sight
spend thrift	tac tics	brim stone	tav ern	for feit
des cant	op tics	san guine	gov ern	pris on
ped ant	rich es	pris tine	stub born	gar den
pend ant	ash es	trib une	check er	mer chant
ver dant	bon fire	land scape	vic ar	doub let
sol emn	o cean	pam phlet	heif er	fore head
col umn	em pire	proph et	friend ship	vine yard
vol ume	um pire	con tract	hard ship	bis cuit
an swer	wel fare	cal dron	pro gramme	coop er
con quer	hard ware	mod ern	wor ship	wa ter
cor sair	wind pipe	lan tern	star light	mawk ish
grand eur	bag pipe	cis tern	mid night	awk ward
phys ics	horn pipe	pat tern	up right	dwarf ish

DICTATION.

The folly of complaining is evident from its utter inutility.
If complaints could rebuild the house consumed by fire, if
complaints could gather again the wealth once scattered, if
complaints could infuse rapidity into the sluggish blood and
retouch the pale, wasted cheek with the rich hue of health,
if complaints could reach the ear of death and recall the loved
lost ones and give their lips the eloquence of love and their
eyes the glance of affection that once thrilled us—then might
a man complain, and his neighbors might not call it foolish.
—CHARLES F. DEEMS.

5

LESSON 99.

WORDS OF THREE SYLLABLES, ACCENTED ON THE FIRST.

me' te or	car' a mel	dy' na mo	in' grow ing
ab di cant	cal i co	en si lage	in ter view
aft er glow	cel lu loid	fab u lous	lim it ed
an gli can	boun ti ful	fer ro type	lob by ist
au to type	cit i zen	fil i gree	lop sid ed
bark an tine	com mun ist	cer tain ly	mi cro phone
bi cy cle	crys tal lite	fox i ness	mon e tize
ca ble gram	cus pi dor	frac tion al	mon i tor
pho no graph	diz zi ly	hand i cap	or phan age
tel e phone	des pot ize	graph o type	an arch ist

LESSON 100.

WORDS OF THREE SYLLABLES, ACCENTED ON THE FIRST.

pop' u lous	sim' ple ton	cu' ri ous	cal' a mus
pro to plasm	ob se quies	fu ri ous	em pha sis
re al ist	prom is es	lu di crous	di o cese
red in gote	com pass es	dan ger ous	pu is sance
stow a way	du te ous	hid e ous	of fi cer
syn di cate	a que ous	in fa mous	lav en der
wa ter ice	du bi ous	co pi ous	prov en der
wa ter shed	te di ous .	se ri ous	cyl in der
west ern most	o di ous	glo ri ous	in te ger
cu ri ous	stu di ous	nu cle us	scav en ger

LESSON 101.

WORDS OF THREE SYLLABLES, ACCENTED ON THE FIRST.

hus' band man	ep' i cure	mi' cro cosm	fu' mi gate
gen tle man	lig a ture	min i mum	me di ate
al der man	sig na ture	pend u lum	me di um
jour ney man	cur va ture	max i mum	o di um
cler gy man	for feit ure	tym pa num	o pi um
coun try man	an ti pode	guar di an	pre mi um
vet er an	rec om pense	cit a del	spo li ate
won der ful	al ka li	in fi del	o pi ate
sor row ful	hem i stich	sen ti nel	o vert ure

LESSON 102.

WORDS OF THREE SYLLABLES, ACCENTED ON THE SECOND.

ge ner' ic	pa cif' ic	dys pep' tic	sa tir' ic
gym nas tic	pa thet ic	ec cen tric	schis mat ic
har mon ic	pe dan tic	ec lec tic	scho las tic
hys ter ic	phleg mat ic	ec stat ic	scor bu tic
i ron ic	as cet ic	e lec tric	so phis tic
in trin sic	ath let ic	em pir ic	stig mat ic
la con ic	au then tic	er rat ic	sym met ric
mag net ic	bar bar ic	fa nat ic	syn od ic
mag nif ic	bo tan ic	fo ren sic	ter rif ic
ma jes tic	clas sif ic	pneu mat ic	the ist ic

LESSON 103.

WORDS OF THREE SYLLABLES, ACCENTED ON THE FIRST.

cream' er y	spu' ri ous	ra' di us	buf' fa lo
pho no gram	lu mi nous	ter mi nus	cred u lous
spec tro scope	glu ti nous	syl la bus	cal i co
but ter scotch	mu ti nous	in cu bus	in di go
skel e ton	ru in ous	ver bi age	ver ti go
tel e gram	gen er al	gas o line	ni hil ist
type wri ter	dy na mite	har bin ger	ped i gree

DICTATION.

Patriotism with an American is a noun personal. It is the American himself and something over. He loves America as he loves himself. He loves her for herself and for himself—because she is America and everything besides. He never gets acclimated elsewhere; he never loses citizenship to the "old home." The right of expatriation is a pure abstraction to him. He may breathe in France, but he lives in America. His treasure is here, and his heart also. If he looks at the Delta of the Nile it reminds him of the Mississippi swamps. He views the dome of St. Paul's with an increased respect for his Capitol at Washington, and listens to the eloquence of Gladstone, or the fiery utterances of Lord Randolph Churchill, with a longing desire to hear our Ransom, or Fowle, or Vance. He is nothing if not patriotic.— EDWARD C. SMITH.

LESSON 104.

WORDS OF THREE SYLLABLES, ACCENTED ON THE FIRST.

n' a gram	ty' po graph	mack' er el	ju' ry man
p i gram	au to graph	cod i cil	gar ni ture
non o gram	par a graph	dom i cile	fur ni ture
li a gram	ep i taph	way far ing	sep ul ture
t ni verse	av e nue	fu gi tive	par a dise
l co hol	rev e nue	nu tri tive	mer chan dise
it ri ol	ret i nue	e go tism	en ter prise
ar a sol	des pot ism	du pli cate	ad ver tise
i ne cure	par ox ysm	ro se ate	hand ker chief

LESSON 105.

WORDS OF THREE SYLLABLES, ACCENTED ON THE SECOND.

ne chan' ic	cos met' ic	po lem' ic	ty ran' nic
no nas tic	di dac tic	pro lif ic	e las tic
u mer ic	do mes tic	pro phet ic	bom bast ic
r gan ic	dog mat ic	rhap sod ic	sta tis tic
s sif ic	dra mat ic	ro man tic	the at ric
or pe do	back gam mon	in cite ment	de po nent
o ot ic	bal mor al	ex cite ment	op po nent
vith draw al	bo nan za	re fine ment	com po nent
r gan ic	pa trol man	con fine ment	ad ja cent
ros pect or	de mean or	e lope ment	in de cent
nag net ic	re main der.	re fresh ment	vice ge rent

LESSON 106.

WORDS OF THREE SYLLABLES, ACCENTED ON THE FIRST.

ad′ jec tive	jew′ el er	ob′ vi ous	sed′ u lous
prim i tive	trav el er	blas phe mous	gran u lous
tran si tive	car a mel	scur ril ous	pend u lous
sen si tive	bur glar ize	mar vel ous	em u lous
sub stan tive	wit ti cism	friv o lous	trem u lous
rel a tive	tri cy cle	fab u lous	pop u lous
nar ra tive	con fer ence	neb u lous	in fa mous
lax a tive	en vi ous	glob u lous	de vi ous
ex ple tive	per vi ous	cred u lous	pre vi ous
neg a tive	per il ous	glan du lous	li bel ous

LESSON 107.

WORDS OF THREE SYLLABLES, ACCENTED ON THE SECOND.

de fend′ ant	ad vance′ ment	re luc′ tant
as cend ant	a merce ment	im por tant
at tend ant	in fringe ment	re sist ant
co her ent	de tach ment	in con stant
ad her ent	at tach ment	in cum bent
in her ent	in trench ment	pu tres cent
im pru dent	re trench ment	de pend ent
pro bos cis	de part ment	in dul gent
el lip sis	ad just ment	re ful gent
syn op sis	in vest ment	ef ful gent
com mand ment	a but ment	e mul gent
a mend ment	trans cend ent	as trin gent

LESSON 108.

WORDS OF THREE SYLLABLES, ACCENTED ON THE LAST.

o ver shoot′	mu ti neer′	fin an cier′	un der go′
in ter cept	pi o neer	brig a dier	o ver leap
in ter rupt	auc tion eer	gren a dier	o ver sleep
dis u nite	o ver seer	bom bar dier	dis ap pear
dis re pute	pri va teer	res er voir	o ver cast
in ter leave	vol un teer	o ver joy	re in vest
in ter weave	gaz et teer	mis em ploy	co ex ist
mis be have	re im burse	es pla nade	pre ex ist
un de ceive	o ver hang	in ex pert	in ter mix
moun tain eer	o ver match	ker o sene	o ver throw
en gi neer	dis em bark	o ver top	o ver flow

DICTATION.

To North Carolina here's my hand, my strongest faith and love,
For it is the noblest land beneath the heavens above;
Then may my trust in Carolina never, never cease—
The bravest of the States in war—the grandest one in peace.

Nature's riches of the soil throughout the State abound,
And in her cloud-land springs of life can everywhere be found;
While peace and plenty reign supreme in cot and palace home,
And joy abides from mountain peaks to ocean's snowy foam.

In education, North Carolina takes the highest stand
Of all the States united in America's proud land;
May Heaven's blessings ever rest on Carolina's name,
While coming ages only add new luster to her fame.

LESSON 109.

WORDS OF THREE SYLLABLES, ACCENTED ON THE FIRST.

por′ cu pine	pol′ y gon	gal′ li cism	mar′ i ner
or i gin	cham pi on	skep ti cism	cor o ner
jav e lin	scor pi on	syl lo gism	can is ter
har le quin	cher u bim	her o ism	min is ter
lex i con	ser a phim	bar ba rism	sin is ter
oc ta gon	mar tyr dom	as ter ism	met a phor
pen ta gon	id i om	aph o rism	bach e lor
hep ta gon	cat a plasm	mag net ism	chan cel lor
hex a gon	os tra cism	bar ris ter	em per or

LESSON 110.

WORDS OF THREE SYLLABLES, ACCENTED ON THE LAST.

leath er et′	as cer tain′	pre ma ture′	mis in form′
pre con ceive	en ter tain	im ma ture	coun ter act
o ver drive	re ap pear	ad ver tise	in di rect
dis ap prove	dis in ter	re com pose	in cor rect
o ver reach	in ter sperse	de com pose	in ter sect
o ver look	ap per tain	in ter pose	con tra dict
dis in thrall	su per vene	pre dis pose	o ver set
re in stall	in ter vene	re in state	in ter mit
mis de mean	im por tune	im po lite	rep re sent
un fore seen	op por tune	re u nite	dis con tent
fore or dain	in se cure	dis af fect	cir cum vent
o ver strain	in ter fere	o ver whelm	pic a yune

LESSON 111.

WORDS OF THREE SYLLABLES, ACCENTED ON THE FIRST.

in' ti mate	sep' a rate	sal' i vate	it' er ate
es ti mate	cel e brate	cul ti vate	em i grate
fas ci nate	des e crate	cap ti vate	des per ate
or di nate	con se crate	ren o vate	as pi rate
ful mi nate	ex e crate	in no vate	dec o rate
nom i nate	ver ber ate	ad e quate	per fo rate
ger mi nate	ul cer ate	fluc tu ate	cor po rate
per son ate	mod er ate	ven er ate	pen e trate
pas sion ate	ag gre gate	op er ate	ar bi trate
for tu nate	ver te brate	as per ate	ac cu rate
dis si pate	gen er ate	trans mi grate	lam i nate

LESSON 112.

WORDS OF THREE SYLLABLES, ACCENTED ON THE FIRST.

in' du rate	lu' cu brate	cir' cu late	sub' li mate
sat u rate	des o late	mod u late	an i mate
sus ci tate	ad vo cate	reg u late	ir ri tate
med i tate	ven ti late	un du late	hes i tate
im i tate	tit il late	em u late	grav i tate
sit u ate	scin til late	stim u late	am pu tate
ex pi ate	per co late	gran u late	ex ca vate
de vi ate	im mo late	stip u late	ag gra vate
vi o late	spec u late	pop u late	grad u ate
ru mi nate	cal cu late	con su late	sal i vate

LESSON 113.

WORDS OF THREE SYLLABLES, ACCENTED ON THE FIRST.

def' i nite	pros' e cute	ves' ti bule	tel' e scope
ap po site	per se cute	rid i cule	an te lope
op po site	ex e cute	hem is phere	pro to type
in fi nite	ab so lute	at mos phere	vol a tile
hyp o crite	dis so lute	com mo dore	ver sa tile
par a site	sub sti tute	syc a more	mer can tile
ob so lete	des ti tute	mus ca dine	in fan tile
ex pe dite	in sti tute	ser pen tine	dis ci pline
sat el lite	con sti tute	tur pen tine	mas cu line
er e mite	pros e lyte	an o dyne	fem i nine
ap pe tite	bar be cue	mi cro scope	fa vor ite

DICTATION.

North Carolina is a land whose perpetual dripping of golden sunbeams makes our severest winters an eternal stranger to those sharp and biting winds which sleep on beds of ice, wrapped in sheets of everlasting snow. It is a land whose bleak December allows the flower-embowered verandas and vine-clad piazzas to remain comfortable enough for lovers to find their sweetest retreat; and there, warmed only by the glimmering fires of falling starbeams, they count the dulcet flight of happiest moments, timed to the rapturous pulsings of their own ecstatic heart-beats as they go ebbing away, freighted with the odor of fragrant flowers, and the melody of birds whose throats are lined with song the whole year through. —W. H. BLOUNT.

LESSON 114.

WORDS OF THREE SYLLABLES, ACCENTED ON THE FIRST.

in' tel lect	es' cu lent	el' e phant	min' u et
cir cum spect	op u lent	sim i lar	im pe tus
pick pock et	vir u lent	pop u lar	cat a ract
lev er et	per ma nent	tab u lar	syc o phant
cat a pult	sup pli cant	glob u lar	pet u lant
men di cant	mis cre ant	sec u lar	ad a mant
in do lent	ter ma gant	oc u lar	cov e nant
tur bu lent	el e gant	ben e fit	con so nant
suc cu lent	lit i gant	al pha bet	per ti nent
fec u lent	ar ro gant	par a pet	tol er ant

LESSON 115.

WORDS OF THREE SYLLABLES, ACCENTED ON THE SECOND.

dic ta' tor	pro vi' so	con fess' or	con ject' ure
tes ta tor	po ta to	ag gress or	de bent ure
en vi ron	oc ta vo	suc cess or	in dent ure
pa go da	sub scrib er	com mix ture	en rap ture
tor pe do	re vi val	con tex ture	con tin ue
bra va do	en dan ger	pre fig ure	for bid ding
tor na do	de ci pher	dis fig ure	un er ring
vi ra go	ma neu ver	trans fig ure	pro ceed ing
a vow al	co e val	co e qual	in cis or
dis loy al	re fu sal	re new al	cre a tor
dis cour age	re pri sal	i de al	spec ta tor

LESSON 116.

WORDS OF THREE SYLLABLES, ACCENTED ON THE FIRST.

ban' ish ment	det' ri ment	bank' rupt cy	sum' ma ry
blan dish ment	sen ti ment	ten den cy	rem e dy
pun ish ment	doc u ment	pun gen cy	com e dy
ped i ment	teg u ment	clem en cy	per fi dy
sed i ment	mon u ment	cur ren cy	mel o dy
com pli ment	nour ish ment	sol ven cy	mon o dy
lin i ment	pol y glot	par a dox	par o dy
mer ri ment	in ter est	cic a trix	pros o dy
an ec dote	res i due	hor o scope	pu er ile

LESSON 117.

WORDS OF FOUR SYLLABLES, ACCENTED ON THE SECOND.

sub treas' u ry	a e' ri al	ap pro' pri ate
ag nos ti cism	an nu i ty	in fu ri ate
ex ag er ate	me mo ri al	al le vi ate
ex as per ate	de mo ni ac	ab bre vi ate
ex am in er	am mo ni ac	an ni hi late
ex ec u tive	e lu ci date	ac cu mu late
ex ec u tor	ad ju di cate	il lu mi nate
ex ec u trix	im me di ate	e nu mer ate
ex em pli fy	re pu di ate	re mu ner ate
ex on er ate	col le gi ate	in cor po rate
pho nog ra phy	ex fo li ate	no ta ri al
pa pyr o graph	in e bri ate	ma te ri al
te leph o ny	ex co ri ate	im pe ri al

LESSON 118.

WORDS OF THREE SYLLABLES, ACCENTED ON THE SECOND.

to bog' gan	al bes' cence	de file' ment	at tain' ment
ma nil la	en tice ment	dis cern ment	en roll ment
com pos ite	en force ment	pre fer ment	ab hor rent
con fec tion	di vorce ment	a mass ment	con cur rent
com mer cial	in duce ment	al lot ment	con sist ent
e lect ive	a gree ment	a part ment	re solv ent
fo ren sic	en gage ment	re tire ment	de lin quent
ag nos tic	im peach ment	ac quire ment	re cum bent
ren coun ter	ap prov al	un e qual	le gu men
es pous al	de part ure	re quit al	tri bu nal
en coun ter	ar ri val	pri me val	a cu men

DICTATION.

'Tis education forms not the common but the uncommon mind. The common mind is the uneducated mind.

Very few of those who consider themselves educated have the inherent faculties of their minds fully brought out.

In many there are latent intellectual powers, unsuspected by others, and unknown to themselves.

That is more than a beautiful fancy, therefore, which runs through Gray's admired "Elegy in a Country Churchyard":

> "Perhaps in this neglected spot is laid
>   Some heart once pregnant with celestial fire;
> Hands that the rod of empire might have swayed,
>   Or waked to ecstacy the living lyre."

JOSEPH M. ATKINSON.

LESSON 119.

WORDS OF THREE SYLLABLES, ACCENTED ON THE SECOND.

re venge′ ful	pro spec′ tive	a bor′ tive	ob ject′ ive
for get ful	per spec tive	di gest ive	e lect ive
e vent ful	cor rect ive	ex pul sive	ad he sive
neg lect ful	in vent ive	com pul sive	co he sive
dis gust ful	per cep tive	im pul sive	de ci sive
dis trust ful	pre sumptive	re pul sive	cor ro sive
suc cess ful	con sump tive	in ac tive	a bu sive
un skill ful	de cep tive	de fect ive	con clu sive
col lect ive	as sert ive	ef fect ive	ex clu sive

LESSON 120.

WORDS OF FOUR SYLLABLES, ACCENTED ON THE SECOND.

ar te′ ri al	gram ma′ ri an	tar ta′ re ous
ar mo ri al	bar ba ri an	com mo di ous
mer cu ri al	in fe ri or	fe lo ni ous
em po ri um	su pe ri or	har mo ni ous
sen so ri um	an te ri or	gra tu i tous
tra pe zi um	pos te ri or	for tu i tous
cri te ri on	ex te ri or	lux u ri ant
cen tu ri on	pro pri e tor	e lu so ry
en co mi um	ex tra ne ous	il lu so ry
tra ge di an	spon ta ne ous	so ci e ty
co me di an	cu ta ne ous	im pu ri ty
col le gi an	er ro ne ous	se cu ri ty
ce ru le an	ter ra que ous	ob scu ri ty

LESSON 121.

WORDS OF THREE SYLLABLES, ACCENTED ON THE SECOND.

com pas' sion	con cus' sion	pro gres' sion
per ver sion	dis cus sion	re gres sion
con ver sion	ac ces sion	pre scrip tion
in ver sion	se ces sion	pro scrip tion
di ver sion	con ces sion	re demp tion
re ver sion	pro ces sion	con sump tion
sub ver sion	con fes sion	a dop tion
a ver sion	pro fes sion	ab sorp tion
dis per sion	ag gres sion	e rup tion
as per sion	di gres sion	cor rup tion

LESSON 122.

WORDS OF FOUR SYLLABLES, ACCENTED ON THE FIRST.

cen' te na ry	spec' u la tive	sta' tion a ry
al co hol ism	nom i na tive	est u a ry
fil i bus ter	op er a tive	mer ce na ry
def al ca tor	fig u ra tive	car i ca ture
dev as ta tor	veg e ta tive	tem per a ture
lam ent a ble	im i ta tive	lit er a ture
kin der gar ten	spir it u ous	ag ri cul ture
he li o type	spir it u al	hor ti cul ture
a er o sphere	lin e a ment	pres by ter y
ju di ca ture	vis ion a ry	des ul to ry
ex pli ca tive	mis sion a ry	prom on to ry
pal li a tive	dic tion a ry	per emp to ry

LESSON 123.

WORDS OF THREE SYLLABLES, ACCENTED ON THE SECOND

in vec' tive	in cen' tive	ex ces' sive	il lu' sive
vin dic tive	re ten tive	pro gres sive	col lu sive
af flic tive	at ten tive	op pres sive	ob tru sive
at trac tive	pre vent ive	ex pres sive	in tru sive
dis tinc tive	de fen sive	im pres sive	pro tru sive
sub junc tive	of fen sive	sub mis sive	e va sive
con junc tive	sub ver sive	per mis sive	per sua sive
in duc tive	dis cur sive	trans mis sive	as sua sive
pro duc tive	ex cur sive	in clu sive	dis sua sive
de struc tive	in cur sive	e lu sive	un fa ding
con struc tive	suc ces sive	de lu sive	ag nos tic
ex ceed ing	en cour age	pe ru sal	il le gal
sub al tern	mo las ses	re ci tal	de ni al

DICTATION.

Who can calculate the value of constitutional united liberty—the blessings of a free press, free schools, and a free
religion? Go and calculate the value of the air we breathe
the water we drink, the earth that we inhabit. By wha
mathematical process will you calculate the value of nationa
character? In what scales will you weigh political equality
and the ballot-box? At what price would you sell American
citizenship? What is self-government worth—its freedom
happiness and example? "Calculate the value of the Union !"
—M. W. RANSOM.

LESSON 124.

WORDS OF THREE SYLLABLES, ACCENTED ON THE SECOND.

le ser′ tion	de duc′ tion	as ser′ tion
n ser tion	re duc tion	ex er tion
e ac tion	se duc tion	con tor tion
on junc tion	in duc tion	dis tor tion
n junc tion	ob struc tion	ex tinc tion
om punc tion	de struc tion	ex ten sion
le coc tion	in struc tion	ex tor tion
on coc tion	con struc tion	ir rup tion
n frac tion	de ten tion	com plex ion
b duc tion	in ten tion	de flux ion

LESSON 125.

WORDS OF FOUR SYLLABLES, ACCENTED ON THE THIRD.

e con struc′ tion	a cous ti′ cian	ad di ca′ tion
es si mist ic	pub li ca tion	ded i ca tion
or gan iz er	rep li ca tion	med i ta tion
p to mist ic	im pli ca tion	in di ca tion
r re spon sive	com pli ca tion	vin di ca tion
l lo path ic	ap pli ca tion	del e ga tion
y clo ra ma	sup pli ca tion	ob li ga tion
yp o der mic	ex pli ca tion	al le ga tion
n tro spec tive	rep ro ba tion	ir ri ga tion
ith o graph ic	ap pro ba tion	lit i ga tion
l lo ca tion	per tur ba tion	mit i ga tion
ev o lu tion	in cu ba tion	in sti ga tion

6

LESSON 126.

WORDS OF FOUR SYLLABLES, ACCENTED ON THE THIRD.

nav i ga′ tion	con ge la′ tion	leg is la′ tion
pro mul ga tion	mu ti la tion	trib u la tion
pro lon ga tion	in stal la tion	pec u la tion
ab ro ga tion ˇ	ap pel la tion	spec u la tion
sub ju ga tion	con stel la tion	cal cu la tion
fas ci na tion	dis til la tion	cir cu la tion
me di a tion	per co la tion	mod u la tion
pal li a tion	vi o la tion	reg u la tion
ex pi a tion	im mo la tion	gran u la tion
va ri a tion	des o la tion	stip u la tion
de vi a tion	con so la tion	pop u la tion
ex ha la tion	con tem pla tion	grat u la tion

DICTATION.

Think not thy worth and work are all unknown
   If not partial penman paint thy praise ;
Man may not see nor mind, but God will own
   Thy worth and labor, thy thoughts and ways.

The desert rose, though never seen by man,
   Is nurtured with a care divinely good ;
The ocean gem, beneath the rolling main,
   Is ever brilliant in the eyes of God.

NEEDHAM BRYAN COBB.

LESSON 127.

WORDS OF THREE SYLLABLES, ACCENTED ON THE SECOND.

de trac' tion	ob jec' tion	com ple' tion	lo ca' tion
con trac tion	pro jec tion	se cre tion	vo ca tion
pro trac tion	e lec tion	con cre tion	gra da tion
dis trac tion	se lec tion	e mo tion	foun da tion
ex trac tion	re flec tion	pro mo tion	cre a tion
con nec tion	plan ta tion	de vo tion	ne ga tion
af fec tion	quo ta tion	pro por tion	mi gra tion
con fec tion	temp ta tion	ces sa tion	ob la tion
per fec tion	pri va tion	no ta tion	re la tion
in fec tion	sal va tion	ro ta tion	trans la tion

LESSON 128.

WORDS OF THREE SYLLABLES, ACCENTED ON THE SECOND.

col lec' tion	re ten' tion	de scrip' tion	at ten' tion
in spec tion	con ten tion	in scrip tion	in ven tion
di rec tion	dis sen sion	sub trac tion	re cep tion
cor rec tion	con ven tion	de pres sion	as crip tion
dis sec tion	de cep tion	im pres sion	ap por tion
de tec tion	con cep tion	op pres sion	ab lu tion
af flic tion	ex cep tion	sup pres sion	so lu tion
re stric tion	per cep tion	ex pres sion	pol lu tion
sub jec tion	e qua tion	li ba tion	for ma tion
de jec tion	vex a tion	pro ba tion	stag na tion
re jec tion	tax a tion	va ca tion	car na tion

LESSON 129.

WORDS OF THREE SYLLABLES, ACCENTED ON THE FIRST.

fel' low ship	sac' ra ment	ten' e ment	mus' cu lar
cal en dar	tes ta ment	part ner ship	reg u lar
vin e gar	man age ment	aq ui line	cel lu lar
in su lar	im ple ment	liq ui date	an nu lar
lig a ment	com ple ment	ped es tal	scap u lar
par lia ment	com pli ment	tu bu lar	spec u lar
fil a ment	bat tle ment	ju gu lar	con su lar
arm a ment	set tle ment	fu ner al	cap su lar

LESSON 130.

WORDS OF THREE SYLLABLES, ACCENTED ON THE FIRST.

tit' u lar	req' ui site	mil' i tant	in' no cent
cim e ter	an nal ist	ad ju tant	ac ci dent
sub lu nar	pes ti lent	rel e vant	in ci dent
can ni bal	prev a lent	prov i dent	in di gent
coch i neal	ex cel lent	pres i dent	neg li gent
mar tin gal	red o lent	dif fi dent	liq ui date
hos pi tal	ig no rant	con fi dent	aq ue duct
eq ui ty	con ver sant	res i dent	liq ue fy

DICTATION.

The mystery rests a mystery still,
        Unsolved of mortal man:
Sphinx-like, untold, the ages hold
        The tale of Cro-a-tan.

MARGARET J. PRESTON.

LESSON 131.

WORDS OF THREE SYLLABLES, ACCENTED ON THE FIRST.

rav' en ous	gen' er ous	haz' ard ous	clam' or ous
om i nous	pros per ous	treach er ous	tim or ous
res in ous	rig or ous	pit e ous	sul phur ous
glut ton ous	nu mer ous	plen te ous	vent ur ous
bar ba rous	o dor ous	im pi ous	rapt ur ous
ul cer ous	hu mor ous	vil lain ous	ar du ous
slan der ous	ri ot ous	vig or ous	mis chiev ous
pon der ous	trai tor ous	val or ous	stren u ous
mur der ous	per vi ous	pre vi ous	sin u ous

LESSON 132.

WORDS OF FOUR SYLLABLES, ACCENTED ON THE SECOND.

ex hor' bi tant	ter res' tri al	e rad' i cate
ex u ber ant	col lat er al	cer tif i cate
ex or di um	de lir i um	in del i cate
cen ten ni al	e ques tri an	pre var i cate
tri en ni al	il lit er ate	ac com mo date
mil len ni al	a dul ter ate	com men su rate
quad ren ni al	as sev er ate	in ves ti gate
per en ni al	e lab o rate	re tal i ate
sep ten ni al	cor rob o rate	de lin e ate
sex ten ni al	in vig o rate	e vap o rate

LESSON 133.

WORDS OF FOUR SYLLABLES, THE FULL ACCENT ON THE
THIRD, AND A SLIGHT ACCENT ON THE FIRST.

liq ue fac′ tion	con ser va′ tor	ev a nes′ cent
liq ue fy ing	des pe ra do	con va les cent
liq ui da tion	mis de mean or	ef flo res cent
req ui si tion	ap pa ra tus	cor res pond ent
pic a yun ish	af fi da vit	in de pend ent
an te ce dent	ex ul ta tion	re im burse ment
dis a gree ment	ad a man tine	dis con tent ment
cir cum ja cent	man u fact ure	om ni pres ent
re en force ment	su per struct ure	in ad vert ent
pre en gage ment	mal e fac tor	pre ex ist ent
en ter tain ment	ben e fac tor	co ex ist ent
in co her ent	met a phys ics	in ter mit tent
in de ci sive	math e mat ics	o ver shad ow
su per vi sor	dis in her it	ac ci dent al

DICTATION.

Chaff is ever with the wheat in the field of the world.
Evil is ever about us and of us, and will be to the end. We
may not be borne to heaven on "flowery beds of ease." In
the moral and spiritual world, as in the natural and physical,
the process of threshing is necessary, and it is *severe*. To
gain and enjoy the victory, the valiant soldier must fight and
"endure hardness." "No cross, no crown."—M. M. MAR-
SHALL.

LESSON 134.

WORDS OF THREE SYLLABLES, ACCENTED ON THE SECOND.

con vic' tion	sus pen' sion	com mis' sion	sen sa' tion
com pul sion	dis sen sion	per mis sion	dic ta tion
ex pul sion	pre ten sion	dis mis sion	ci ta tion
con vul sion	sub mer sion	vi bra tion	di lu tion
ex pan sion	e mer sion	nar ra tion	at trac tion
as cen sion	im mer sion	pros tra tion	re frac tion
de scen sion	pos ses sion	du ra tion	ad mis sion
di men sion	sub mis sion	pul sa tion	re mis sion

LESSON 135.

WORDS OF FOUR SYLLABLES, ACCENTED ON THE SECOND.

lux u' ri ous	trans par' en cy	sa lu' bri ous
vo lu mi nous	al lu vi on	im pe ri ous
o be di ent	pe tro le um	mys te ri ous
ex pe di ent	ce ru le an	la bo ri ous
in gre di ent	le vi a than	in glo ri ous
im mu ni ty	li bra ri an	cen so ri ous
com mu ni ty	pre ca ri ous	vic to ri ous
im pu ni ty	vi ca ri ous	no to ri ous
com pla cen cy	ne fa ri ous	in ju ri ous
e vac u ate	per pet u ate	ex pos tu late
at ten u ate	as sas sin ate	ex hil a rate
ex ten u ate	in dic a tive	o rig i nate
ob lit er ate	in ad e quate	ca pit u late

LESSON 136.

WORDS OF SEVEN SYLLABLES.

im per me a bil′ i ty

rec on cil′ i a to ry

im pon der a bil′ i ty

im ma te ri al′ i ty

in di vid u al′ i ty

per pen dic u lar′ i ty

an te trin i ta′ ri an

val e tu di na′ ri an

con tem po ra′ ne ous ly

ex tem po ra′ ne ous ly

as so ci a′ tion al ism

in di vis i bil′ i ty

in com pat i bil′ i ty

in el i gi bil′ i ty

im per cep ti bil′ i ty

in de struct i bil′ i ty

in de fen si bil′ i ty

in com press i bil′ i ty

im mal le a bil′ i ty

in com bus ti bil′ i ty

ir re sist i bil′ i ty

hu man i ta′ ri an ism

WORDS OF EIGHT SYLLABLES.

un in tel li gi bil′ i ty

in com pre hen si bil′ i ty

DICTATION.

All-shadowing Pilot! high, lone and cold
  Thou rear'st thy form in grandeur, and the light
Which gilds thy brow at sunset, as of old,
  Shall be to thee a diadem all bright,
Amid the ages distant and untold,
  To guide the pilgrim's grim and failing sight
Along thy battlements. And now the sun
Goes down behind the mountains—day is gone.

JAMES B. SHEPARD.

LESSON 137.

WORDS OF FOUR SYLLABLES, ACCENTED ON THE SECOND.

as sim′ i late   con tam′ i nate   pre rog′ a tive
prog nos ti cate   dis sem i nate   ir rel a tive
per am bu late   re crim i nate   ap pel la tive
ap prox i mate   a bom i nate   e jac u late
sub or di nate   in tem per ate   im mac u late
o rig i nate   re gen er ate   ma tric u late
pro cras ti nate   co op er ate   ges tic u late
pre des ti nate   ex as per ate   in oc u late
com pas sion ate   com mis er ate   co ag u late
dis pas sion ate   in vet er ate   de pop u late
pre dom i nate   re it er ate   con grat u late

LESSON 138.

WORDS OF FOUR SYLLABLES, ACCENTED ON THE THIRD.

bi o graph′ ic   hy per bol′ ic   syc o phant′ ic
cab a list ic   hy po stat ic   syl lo gist ic
cas u ist ic   hy po thet ic   sym pa thet ic
cat e chet ic   id i ot ic   sys tem at ic
cat e gor ic   in e las tic   tal is man ic
chro no log ic   math e mat ic   the o log ic
dem o crat ic   met a phor ic   the o crat ic
di a bol ic   met a phys ic   the o ret ic
di a lec tic   myth o log ic   to po graph ic
dip lo mat ic   or tho graph ic   ty po graph ic
di a met ric   pan the ist ic   zo o log ic
di u ret ic   sci en tif ic   ge o cen tric

LESSON 139.

WORDS OF FIVE SYLLABLES, ACCENTED ON THE FOURTH.

an ti scor bu′ tic	gen e a log′ ic	lex i co graph′ i
ar is to crat ic	en thu si as tic	mon o syl lab i
char ac ter is tic	en to mo log ic	or ni tho log ic

DICTATION.

The Wind King from the North came down
Nor stopped by river, mount, or town;
But, like a boisterous god at play,
Resistless, bounding on his way,
He shook the lake and tore the wood,
And flapped his wings in merry mood:
Nor furled them, till he spied afar
The white caps flash on Hatteras Bar,
Where fierce Atlantic landward bowls
O'er treacherous sands and hidden shoals.

Can mortal tongue in song convey
The fury of that fearful fray?
How ships were splintered at a blow—
Sails shivered into shreds of snow,
And seamen hurled to death below!
Two gods commingling bolt and blast,
The huge waves at each other cast
And bellowed o'er the raging waste;
Then sped like harnessed steeds afar
That drag a shattered battle-car
Amid the midnight din of war!

JOSEPH W. HOLDEN.

LESSON 140.

WORDS OF FOUR SYLLABLES, ACCENTED ON THE SECOND.

n tem' pla tive	in dem' ni fy	af fec' tion ate
t per la tive	per son i fy	de lib er ate
ter na tive	re stor a tive	in car cer ate
e clar a tive	dis qual i fy	con fed er ate
m par a tive	un for tu nate	con sid er ate
n per a tive	e man ci pate	pre pon der ate
t de cen cy	gre ga ri ous	pe nu ri ous
i plo ma cy	op pro bri ous	u su ri ous
lem ni ty	ne ces si ty	a cad e my
a ter ni ty	i den ti ty	e con o my
ter ni ty	zo ol o gy	plu toc ra cy

LESSON 141.

WORDS OF FOUR SYLLABLES, ACCENTED ON THE SECOND.

ro lix' i ty	com pul' so ry	su prem' a cy
n cer tain ty	ol fac to ry	the oc ra cy
n mod est y	re frac to ry	de moc ra cy
is hon est y	re fec to ry	con spir a cy
t lil o quy	di rec to ry	ge og ra phy
u man i ty	i dol a try	bi og ra phy
men i ty	ge om e try	ste nog ra phy
t ren i ty	im men si ty	zo og ra phy
i cin i ty	pro pen si ty	to pog ra phy
f fin i ty	ver bos i ty	ty pog ra phy
i vin i ty	ad ver si ty	hy drog ra phy
t dem ni ty	di ver si ty	phi los o phy

LESSON 142.

WORDS OF FOUR SYLLABLES, ACCENTED ON THE THIRD.

par a lyt' ic	em blem at' ic	eq ui ta' ble
par a phrast ic	en er get ic	ac a dem ic
par a sit ic	e nig mat ic	al chem ist ic
par en thet ic	ep i lep tic	al pha bet ic
par a bol ic	ep i dem ic	ap o plet ic
path o log ic	ep i sod ic	an a lyt ic
pe ri od ic	eu cha rist ic	an a tom ic
phil o log ic	ex e get ic	ap os tol ic
phil o soph ic	ge o log ic	a rith me tic
phil an throp ic	ge o met ric	as tro log ic
prob lem at ic	hem is pher ic	as tro nom ic
pu ri tan ic	his tri on ic	a the ist ic
pyr a mid ic	hyp o crit ic	at mos pher ic
pyr o tech nic	eq ui ta bly	bar o met ric

DICTATION.

All hail to thee, our good old State, the noblest of the band
Who raised the flag of liberty in this our native land!
All hail to thee! thy worthy sons were first to spurn the
    yoke;
The tyrant's fetters from thy hands at Mecklenburg they
    broke.   •
No coward foresight they possess'd, on peril's brink to pause
Nor waited for a sister State to lead in freedom's cause.

                                        MARY BAYARD CLARKE.

LESSON 143.

WORDS OF FOUR SYLLABLES, ACCENTED ON THE SECOND.

do cil' i ty · · · hos til' i ty · · · cu pid' i ty
gil i ty · · · tran quil li ty · · · tur gid i ty
ra gil i ty · · · ser vil i ty · · · va lid i ty
hi hil i ty · · · pro pin qui ty · · · so lid i ty
hu mil i ty · · · ca lam i ty · · · ti mid i ty
ste ril i ty · · · ex trem i ty · · · hu mid i ty
vi ril i ty · · · sub lim i ty · · · ra pid i ty
scur ril i ty · · · prox im i ty · · · stu pid i ty
duc til i ty · · · con form i ty · · · a rid i ty
gen til i ty · · · e nor mi ty · · · flo rid i ty
fer til i ty · · · ur ban i ty · · · fe cun di ty

LESSON 144.

WORDS OF FOUR SYLLABLES, ACCENTED ON THE SECOND.

un nat' u ral · · · mil len' ni um · · · neu tral' i ty
con viv i al · · · dis sim i lar · · · in solv en cy
di ag o nal · · · ver nac u lar · · · de lin quen cy
pen tag o nal · · · par tic u lar · · · mo not o ny
tra di tion al · · · ir reg u lar · · · a pos ta sy
in ten tion al · · · bi valv u lar · · · hy poc ri sy
per pet u al · · · re al i ty · · · im pi e ty
ha bit u al · · · le gal i ty · · · va ri e ty
e vent u al · · · re gal i ty · · · so bri e ty
un mer ci ful · · · fru gal i ty · · · pro pri e ty
fa nat i cism · · · for mal i ty · · · sa ti e ty

LESSON 145.

WORDS OF FOUR SYLLABLES, ACCENTED ON THE SECOND.

con cav' i ty	bar bar' i ty	a nat' o my
de prav i ty	dis par i ty	e piph a ny
lon gev i ty	ce leb ri ty	phi lan thro py
ac cliv i ty	a lac ri ty	mis an thro py
na tiv i ty	sin cer i ty	pe riph e ry
cap tiv i ty	ce ler i ty	ar til ler y
fes tiv i ty	te mer i ty	hy drop a thy
per plex i ty	in teg ri ty	de liv er y

LESSON 146.

WORDS OF FOUR SYLLABLES, ACCENTED ON THE SECOND

ex tem' po re	a nal' y sis	im mor' tal ize
dis com fit ure	de lir i ous	pa rish ion er
dis con so late	in dus tri ous	di am e ter
a pos to late	il lus tri ous	ad min is ter
ob se qui ous	las civ i ous	am bas sa dor
oc ca sion al	ob liv i ous	pro gen i tor
pro por tion al	a nom a lous	com pos i tor
un pop u lar	e pit o mize	me trop o lis

DICTATION.

When will the nation's history do justice to North Caro
lina? Never until some faithful and loving son of her own
shall gird his loins to the task, with unwearied industry and
unflinching devotion to the honor of his dear old mother.—
GEORGE DAVIS.

LESSON 147.

WORDS OF FOUR SYLLABLES, ACCENTED ON THE SECOND.

com mand' e ry   te leg' ra pher   con spic' u ous
ca pit u lar   in cred u lous   pro mis cu ous
bi ol o gy   ad vent ur ous   as sid u ous
au ric u lar   a non y mous   am big u ous
ab ir ri gate   un gen er ous   con tig u ous
e lec tro phone   mag nan i mous   mel lif lu ous
li no le um   u nan i mous   su per flu ous
i de al ist   as par a gus   in tel li gent
he red i ty   pre cip i tous   ma lev o lent
ho mog ra phy   ne ces si tous   be nev o lent
sci op ti con   am phib i ous   pre dic a ment

LESSON 148.

WORDS OF FOUR SYLLABLES, ACCENTED ON THE SECOND.

re pub' li can   mi rac' u lous   dis par' age ment
plu toc ra cy   a nal o gous   en cour age ment
phe nom e nal   per fid i ous   en fran chise ment
pa pyr o graph   fas tid i ous   dis fran chise ment
o rig i nal   in sid i ous   en tan gle ment
e lec tro poise   in vid i ous   ac knowl edg ment
con ject ur al   ex or di um   as cend en cy
cen trip e tal   me rid i an   de spond en cy
con tin u al   ob liv i on   e mer gen cy
ef fect u al   in cog ni to   in clem en cy
ju rid i cal   co part ner ship   con sist en cy

LESSON 149.

WORDS OF FOUR SYLLABLES, ACCENTED ON THE SECOND.

ro tun' di ty   in teg' ri ty   fi del' i ty
com mod i ty   ma jor i ty   sta bil i ty
ab surd i ty   pri or i ty   mo bil i ty
lo cal i ty   mi nor i ty   no bil i ty
vo cal i ty   plu ral i ty   fa cil i ty
as per i ty   fa tal i ty   an tiq ui ty
se ver i ty   vi tal i ty   in iq ui ty
pros per i ty   mo ral i ty   u biq ui ty
aus ter i ty   mor tal i ty   in iq ui tous
dex ter i ty   bru tal i ty   am big u ous

LESSON 150.

WORDS OF FOUR SYLLABLES, ACCENTED ON THE SECOND.

in ac' cu rate   prog nos' ti cate   de riv' a tive
ca pac i tate   in tox i cate   de mon stra tive
re sus ci tate   re cip ro cate   con serv a tive
de bil i tate   e quiv o cate   de fin i tive
fa cil i tate   in val i date   in fin i tive
de cap i tate   con sol i date   re trib u tive
pre cip i tate   in tim i date   a mass a ble
in def i nite   di lap i date   de mon e tize
au then ti cate   con cil i ate   bi met al ism
do mes ti cate   ca lum ni ate   ag nos ti cism
con vex i ty   dis til ler ry   dis cov er y
tri an gu lar   a pos ta tize   e phem e ris

LESSON 151.

WORDS OF FOUR SYLLABLES, ACCENTED ON THE SECOND.

es tab' lish ment	im per' ti nent	tem pest' u ous
em bel lish ment	in dif fer ent	sig nif i cant
ac com plish ment	ir rev er ent	ex trav a gant
as ton ish ment	om nip o tent	pre dom i nant
re lin quish ment	mel lif lu ent	in tol er ant
im ped i ment	cir cum flu ent	i tin er ant
ha bil i ment	ac cou ter ments	in hab it ant
im pris on ment	com mu ni cant	ir rel e vant
em bar rass ment	in ge ni ous	be nef i cent
in teg u ment	con tin u ous	mag nif i cent
e mol u ment	in con gru ous	mu nif i cent
pre em i nent	im pet u ous	co in ci dent
in con ti nent	tu mult u ous	im prov i dent

DICTATION.

In this fair, sunny Southern land,
    Where peace and joy and mirth
Reign supreme on every hand,
    Glad Freedom had her birth.

And of the States which make this land
    So brave, so free and great,
No one will ever higher stand
    Than our grand "Old North State."

7

LESSON 152.

WORDS OF FIVE SYLLABLES, ACCENTED ON THE SECOND.

de clam′ a to ry
ex clam a to ry
in flam ma to ry
ex plan a to ry
de clar a to ry
pre par a to ry
ob serv a to ry
con serv a to ry

pre mon′ i to ry
sub serv i en cy
de gen er a cy
con fed er a cy
ef fem i na cy
in hab it an cy
ac com pa ni ment
pro hib it o ry

co op′ er a tive
de rog a to ry
ap pel la to ry
con sol a to ry
de fam a to ry
sub sid i a ry
in cen di a ry
sti pen di a ry

LESSON 153.

WORDS OF FIVE SYLLABLES, ACCENTED ON THE THIRD.

e qui pon′ der ate
par ti cip i al
in di vid u al
in ef fect u al
in tel lect u al
pu sil lan i mous
dis in gen u ous
in sig nif i cant
e qui pon der ant
cir cum am bi ent

par lia ment′ a ry
tes ta ment a ry
sup ple ment a ry
al bu min i form
ho mo ge ne ous
ac ri mo ni ous
par si mo ni ous
dis pro por tion ate
in de ter mi nate
cos mo pol i tan

cer e mo′ ni al
mat ri mo ni al
pat ri mo ni al
an ti mo ni al
tes ti mo ni al
im ma te ri al
mag is te ri al
min is te ri al
im me mo ri al
sen a to ri al

LESSON 154.

WORDS OF FIVE SYLLABLES, ACCENTED ON THE SECOND.

con fec' tion er y	ma te' ri al ist	e pis' to la ry
un nec es sa ry	spas mod i cal ly	vo cab u la ry
he red i ta ry	co tem po ra ry	im ag i na ry
in vol un ta ry	ex tem po ra ry	pre lim i na ry
re sid u a ry	dis pen sa to ry	le git i ma cy
tu mul tu a ry	in vet er a cy	re pos i to ry
ac cent u a tion	un mer chant a ble	in del i ca cy

DICTATION.

North Carolinians cannot forget the past. Around their history cluster memories of lofty patriotism and unsullied honor, of noble daring and high emprise. We do not believe that under heaven's canopy there dwell a people who are more heartily devoted to civil and religious freedom than are our people. They know well what sufferings and trials were encountered before freedom was established within our borders. They remember Liberty's birth-hour, amid perils and darkness—how she was born literally on an open field of battle and blood, amid hissing bullets and dying groans; they remember how fiery storms beat long on her unsheltered and helpless childhood; they remember how, for one hundred years, she has been the guardian angel of the Republic; that under her beneficent protection and favor the thirteen infant colonies have grown into forty-four giant States!—T. B. KINGSBURY.

LESSON 155.

WORDS OF FIVE SYLLABLES, ACCENTED ON THE THIRD.

in de scrib' a bly   si mul ta' ne ous   val e dic' to ry
mel an cho li a   in stan ta ne ous   a re om e try
spon ta ne i ty   al i ment a ry   del e te ri ous
e lec tric i ty   dic ta to ri al   mer i to ri ous
con tra dic to ry   an ni ver sa ry   dis o be di ent
in tro duc to ry   e qua to ri al   in ex pe di ent
trig o nom e try   in ar tic u late   con ti nu i ty
mis cel la ne ous   il le git i mate   im pro pri è ty
sub ter ra ne ous   e le men ta ry   au dit o ri um
suc ce da ne ous   sat is fac to ry   in ter me di ate

LESSON 156.

WORDS OF FIVE SYLLABLES, ACCENTED ON THE THIRD.

in si pid' i ty   in e qual' i ty   an i mos' i ty
il le gal i ty   sen su al i ty   gen er os i ty
prod i gal i ty   u na nim i ty   flex i bil i ty
cor di al i ty   in hu man i ty   im mo bil i ty
per son al i ty   ar is toc ra cy   sol u bil i ty
prin ci pal i ty   in ad ver ten cy   vol u bil i ty
lib er al i ty   reg u lar i ty   mag na nim i ty
gen er al i ty   pop u lar i ty   phra se ol o gy
im mo ral i ty   me di oc ri ty   os te ol o gy
hos pi tal i ty   in sin cer i ty   no to ri e ty
im mor tal i ty   cu ri os i ty   a er ol o gy

LESSON 157.

WORDS OF FIVE SYLLABLES, ACCENTED ON THE THIRD.

im por tu′ ni ty	dis a bil′ i ty	in ci vil′ i ty
op por tu ni ty	in sta bil i ty	u ni form i ty
per pe tu i ty	mu ta bil i ty	non con form i ty
punct u al i ty	cred i bil i ty	con san guin i ty
mut u al i ty	tan gi bil i ty	sin gu lar i ty
in fi del i ty	so cia bil i ty	joc u lar i ty
prob a bil i ty	tract a bil i ty	in ter na tion al
in a bil i ty	pla ca bil i ty	klep to ma ni ac
du ra bil i ty	in u til i ty	am bi gu i ty

DICTATION.

Would you gather a garland of beauty bright?
You should wander at dawn or by pale moonlight,
While the breeze is fresh on the opening flowers,
Or their leaves are moist with the dewy showers;
One Rose you should gather, and gladly entwine her,
The soft-opening Rose-bud of North Carolina.

Nay, go where you will, over mountain or plain,
In country or city where gay fashions reign,
Wherever Columbia's daughters are found,
Fair blossoms of beauty are scattered around,
But yet there is one, among all much finer,
The fresh-blooming Rose-bud of North Carolina.

ROBERT STRANGE.

LESSON 158.

WORDS OF FIVE SYLLABLES, ACCENTED ON THE THIRD.

con ti gu' i ty	con ti nu' i ty	plau si bil' i ty
an æs the si a	in ge nu i ty	im be cil i ty
su per flu i ty	in con gru i ty	in do cil i ty
in cre du li ty	fal li bil i ty	vol a til i ty
in se cu ri ty	fea si bil i ty	ver sa til i ty
im ma tu ri ty	vis i bil i ty	ca pa bil i ty
per spi cu i ty	sen si bil i ty	at trac tiv i ty
as si du i ty	pos si bil i ty	dip so ma ni ac

LESSON 159.

WORDS OF SIX SYLLABLES, ACCENTED ON THE FOURTH.

ma te ri al' i ty	com bus ti bil' i ty	in ca pa bil' i ty
il lib er al i ty	ir reg u lar i ty	pen e tra bil i ty
u ni ver sal i ty	in fe ri or i ty	in sen si bil i ty
in hos pi tal i ty	su pe ri or i ty	im pos si bil i ty
in stru men tal i ty	im pet u os i ty	in cred i bil i ty
spir it u al i ty	gen er al is si mo	im mu ta bil i ty
im prob a bil i ty	dis ci pli na ri an	il leg i bil i ty
im pla ca bil i ty	pre des ti na ri an	re fran gi bil i ty
mal le a bil i ty	an te di lu vi an	in fal li bil i ty
in flam ma bil i ty	het e ro ge ne ous	di vis i bil i ty
com press i bil i ty	me di a to ri al	par tic u lar i ty
com pat i bil i ty	o le o mar ga rine	dis sim i lar i ty
de struct i bil i ty	de cal co ma ni a	in flex i bil i ty
per cep ti bil i ty	hu man i ta ri an	re sist i bil i ty

LESSON 160.

WORDS OF IRREGULAR ORTHOGRAPHY.

ghost	folks	ma′ ny	is′ land	tomb
corps	ra′ tio	ba teau′	does	wolf
ache	va lise′	beau	says	yacht
half	o′ cean	beaux	said	dough
calf	though	bu′ reau	lieu	neigh
calve	broad	been	a dieu′	sleigh
one	could	bu′ ry	debt	weigh
once	would	bu′ ri al	phlegm	gauge
done	should	bus′ y	croup	bough
gone	a′ ny	isle	doubt	slough

DICTATION.

Speech is the deliverer of the imprisoned soul. It opens the portals of the heart and invites thought and emotion forth into light and liberty. As another has beautifully said: "Words reaching from the speaker's tongue to the listener's ear are the links of that golden chain upon which thought flies from mind to mind, and feeling from heart to heart."

Speech, however, derives its most permanent value from its written exponent. The achievements of the past, the wisdom, wit and beauty of other days would have remained buried in the tomb of the Capulets forever had not

> "Letters evoked their ghosts,
> And kept the pale embodied shades
> From fleshless lips to warn us."

THOMAS H. PRITCHARD.

LESSON 161.

WORDS OF IRREGULAR ORTHOGRAPHY.

flam' beau	bus' i ly	beau' ty	pi' quant
right' eous	colonel	beau' te ous	pi' quan cy
in veigh'	gui tar'	ca noe'	sol' dier
wom' an	su' gar	plaid	vict' uals
wom' en	vis' count	schism	bou quet'
bis' cuit	ap ro pos'	hal' cy on	bru nette'
cir' cuit	ugh	mis' tle toe	ga zette'
sal' mon	co quette'	psal' mo dy	in debt' ed
isth' mus	cro quet'	bal sam' ic	lieu ten' ant
bus' i ness	mort' gage	neigh' bor	qua drille'

LESSON 162.

g AND *k* BEFORE *n* ARE ALWAYS SILENT.

gnat	knap' weed	knight' hood	knot' ty
gnaw	knell	knight' ly	knot' ti ly
gnome	knave	knit	knot' ti ness
gnarl	knav' er y	knit' ter	knout
gnash	knav' ish	knit' ting	know
gnos' tics	knav' ish ly	knob	know' a ble
gnos' ti cism	knav' ish ness	knob' by	known
knab	knead	knock	know' ing
knack	knee	knock' er	know' ing ly
knag	kneel	knoll	knowl' edge
knag' gy	knife	knot	knuck' le
knap	knight	knot' grass	knurl
knap' sack	knight er' rant	knot' ted	knurl' y

LESSON 163.

WORDS OF IRREGULAR ORTHOGRAPHY.

cap u chin′	fas cine′	re sign′	des ig na′ tion
mag a zine′	fron′ tier	im pugn′	res ig na′ tion
sub ma rine′	chaise	op pugn′	ma lig′ nant
bom ba zine′	cha grin′	ar raign′	in dig′ ni ty
brig a dier′	cham paign′	coun′ ter sign	in dig′ nant
can non ier′	chi cane′	con dign′	dig′ ni ty
cap a pie′	chi can′ er y	be nign′	dig′ ni fy
car bin ier′	chev a lier′	poign′ ant	op pug′ nan cy
cav a lier′	chiv′ al ry	for′ eign	re pug′ nant
quar an tine′	chan de lier′,	sov′ er eign	re pug′ nan cy
man da rin′	sign	en′ sign	sig′ ni fy
cash ier′	as sign′	cam paign′	sig nif i ca′ tion
ma rine′	con sign′	be nig′ nant	feign
ca price′	de sign′	be nig′ ni ty	deign
po lice′	ma lign′	ma lig′ ni ty	reign

DICTATION.

"Swannanoa, nymph of beauty,
  I would woo thee in my rhyme;
Wildest, brightest, loveliest river
  Of our sunny, Southern clime!
Swannanoa, well they named thee,
  In the mellow Indian tongue;
Beautiful thou art, most truly,
  And right worthy to be sung."

LESSON 164.

WORDS OF IRREGULAR ORTHOGRAPHY.

il log' ic al	do min' i cal	con cen' tric	me tal' lic
in im' i cal	com' ic al	e le' gi ac	pleth' o ric
me thod' ic al	met' ri cal	ec stat' ic	car bol' ic
far' ci cal	phys' ic al	ep' ic	sul phu' ri
med' i cal	prac' ti cal	ex ot' ic	plas' tic
trop' ic al	rad' i cal	ap o stroph' ic	pub' lic
top' ic al	ver' ti cal	chol' er ic	re pub' lic
bib' li cal	vor' ti cal	lu' na tic	tac' tic
ca non' ic al	whim' si cal	gal' lic	arc' tic
chi mer' ic al	quad rat' ic	hym' nic	pep' tic
cler' ic al	cath' o lic	i tal' ic	e las' tic
cos' mi cal	ce phal' ic	me dal' lic	cys' tic
cor' ti cal	cha ot' ic	me te or' ic	car bon' ic

LESSON 165.

WORDS OF IRREGULAR ORTHOGRAPHY.

balk	cough	rhu' barb	calm
calk	trough	rhet' o ric	calm' ly
chalk	laugh	rhap' so dy	calm' ness
stalk	through	rhi noc' e ros	be calm'
talk	plough	alms' giv ing	psalm
walk	though	alms' house	qualm
tough	rheum	alms	qualm' ish
rough	rheu mat' ic	em balm'	psalm' ist
slough	rheu' ma tism	balm' y	blud' geon
e nough'	rhyme	balm	dud' geon

LESSON 166.

WORDS ENDING IN *ize.*

au' thor ize
civ' il ize
can' on ize
le' gal ize
sub' sid ize
tyr' an nize
sys' tem ize
meth' od ize
jour' nal ize
bru' tal ize
col' o nize
en' er gize

mor' al ize
dram' a tize
em' pha size
gal' van ize
her' bo rize
or' gan ize
pat' ron ize
sat' ir ize
tan' tal ize
vo' cal ize
cau' ter ize
bar' bar ize

mag' net ize
mod' ern ize
ag' o nize
pul' ver ize
ster' il ize
dram' a tize
fer' til ize
i' dol ize
mel' o dize
mes' mer ize
po' lar ize
re' al ize

LESSON 167.

e' qual ize
hu' man ize
al' co hol ize
al' le go rize
a nath' e ma tize
an' i mal ize
e pis' to lize
bes' tial ize
e nig' ma tize
char' ac ter ize
e the' re al ize

bot' a nize
dog' ma tize
gen' er al ize
lib' er al ize
ma te' ri al ize
me mo' ri al ize
min' er al ize
mo nop' o lize
nat' u ral ize
ox' y gen ize
par tic' u lar ize

the' o rize
tran' quil ize
tem' po rize
pan' e gy rize
pop' u lar ize
pros' e lyt ize
pu' ri tan ize
re pub' lic an ize
sec' u lar ize
sen' su al ize
spir' it u al ize

LESSON 168.

WORDS IN WHICH *ci* AND *ti* ARE SOUNDED AS *sh.*

sus pi′ cious	ap po si′ tion	av a ri′ cious
suf fi′ cient	eb ul li′ tion	in au spi′ cious
vo li′ tion	er u di′ tion	ben e fi′ cial
ab o li′ tion	ex hi bi′ tion	co a li′ tion
ac qui si′ tion	im po si′ tion	com pe ti′ tion
ad mo ni′ tion	op po si′ tion	com po si′ tion
ad ven ti′ tious	prej u di′ cial	def i ni′ tion
am mu ni′ tion	pol i ti′ cian	dem o li′ tion
pre mo ni′ tion	prep o si′ tion	dep o si′ tion
dis qui si′ tion	prop o si′ tion	dis po si′ tion
in qui si′ tion	pro hi bi′ tion	prac ti′ tion er
rep e ti′ tion	su per fi′ cial	a rith me ti′ cian
in hi bi′ tion	su per sti′ tion	ac a de mi′ cian
ex po si′ tion	sup po si′ tion	ge om e tri′ cian
ap pa ri′ tion	sur rep ti′ tious	in ju di′ cious
ar ti fi′ cial	mer e tri′ cious	de fi′ cien cy

DICTATION.

Words fail to depict the grandeur of this people, if, with the opening development of our material wealth, and the dotting of our plains and mountains with new homes, and the filling of our ports with the commerce of the seas, we shall faithfully cling to the virtues that make man master of circumstances. To perpetuate the virtues of the father is to guard the future of the children.—CLAUD B. DENSON.

LESSON 169.

WORDS IN WHICH *ce, ci, ti* AND *si* ARE SOUNDED AS *sh*.

sub stan' tial	fe ro' cious	li cen' tious
con fi den' tial	lo qua' cious	in cau' tious
pen i ten' tial	ra pa' cious	ef fi ca' cious
prov i den' tial	sa ga' cious	os ten ta' tious
rev er en' tial	te na' cious	per spi ca' cious
e qui noc' tial	vex a' tious	per ti na' cious
in flu en' tial	vi va' cious	con sci en' tious
pes ti len' tial	vo ra' cious	pa' tient
au da' cious	ve ra' cious	quo' tient
ca pa' cious	crus ta' ceous	an' cient
fa ce' tious	con ten' tious	tran' sient

LESSON 170.

fal la' cious	in fec' tious	par ti al' i ty
a tro' cious	sen ten' tious	im par ti al' i ty
pre' cious	mo ni' tion	ma gi' cian
spe' cial	mu ni' tion	ma li' cious
vi' cious	con tri' tion	mi li' tia
ad di' tion	at tri' tion	mu si' cian
am bi' tion	nu tri' tion	of fi' cial
aus pi' cious	cog ni' tion	pa tri' cian
of fi' cious	ig ni' tion	par ti' tion
ca pri' cious	con di' tion	per di' tion
nu tri' tious	de fi' cient	per ni' cious
de li' cious	de li' cious	pe ti' tion

LESSON 171.

WORDS IN WHICH *ce, ci, ti* AND *si* ARE SOUNDED AS *sh*.

gra' cious	par' tial	an nun' ci ate	fac ti' tous
spa' cious	es sen' tial	li cen' ti ate	fic ti' tious
spe' cious	po ten' tial	sub stan' ti ate	den ti' tion
spe' cies	pro vin' cial	no vi' ti ate	fru i' tion
so' cial	pru den' tial	of fi' ci ate	es pe' cial
gen' tian	com mer' cial	ex cru' ci ate	op ti' cian
ter' tian	im par' tial	pro pi' ti ate	dis cre' tion
con' science	as so' ci ate	e nun' ci ate	e di' tion
cap' tious	con so' ci ate	de nun' ci ate	ef fi' cient
fac' tious	ap pre' ci ate	dis so' ci ate	fla gi' tious
fic' tious	de pre' ci ate	sa' ti ate	ju di' cial
lus' cious	e ma' ci ate	vi' ti ate	lo gi' cian
frac' tious	ex pa' ti ate	pro fi' cient	po si' tion
cau' tious	in gra' ti ate	phy si' cian	se di' tion

LESSON 172.

WORDS OF IRREGULAR ORTHOGRAPHY.

stur' geon	con ta' gious	sac ri le' gious	mosque
le' gion	e gre' gious	plague	in trigue'
re' gion	re li' gious	vague	o paque'
con ta' gion	pro di' gious	league	u nique'
re li' gion	punch' eon	brogue	pique
sur' geon	trunch' eon	rogue	har angue'
dun' geon	scutch' eon	fa tigue'	ap' o logue
pig' eon	es cutch' eon	vogue	cat' a logue
lunch' eon	gor' geous	tongue	di' a logue

LESSON 173.

IN THE FOLLOWING, *c* OR *g* ENDING A SYLLABLE HAVING A PRIMARY OR SECONDARY ACCENT, IS SOUNDED AS *s* AND *j* RESPECTIVELY.

ac′ it	mag′ ic	pac′ i fy
g′ i tate	trag′ ic	reg′ i cide
eg′ i ble	ag′ ile	reg′ i men
rig′ i lant	ac′ id	reg′ is ter
eg′ i ment	dig′ it	spec′ i fy
rec′ e dent	fac′ ile	mac′ er ate
rec′ i pice	frag′ ile	mag′ is trate
ec′ i pe	frig′ id	mag′ is tra cy
lec′ i mal	rig′ id	trag′ e dy
lec′ i mate	plac′ id	vic′ i nage

LESSON 174.

ac′ er ate	vig′ il	au then tic′ i ty
ar tic′ i pate	veg′ e tate	e las tic′ i ty
im plic′ i ty	veg′ e ta ble	du o dec′ i mo
ne dic′ i nal	log′ ic	in ca pac′ i tate
o lic′ i tude	proc′ ess	ab o rig′ i nal
ri plic′ i ty	cog′ i tate	ec cen tric′ i ty
er tic′ i ty	prog′ e ny	vac′ il la to ry
us tic′ i ty	il lic′ it	mu ci lag′ i nous
x ag′ ger ate	im plic′ it	mul ti plic′ i ty
nor dac′ i ty	e lic′ it	per ti nac′ i ty

LESSON 175.

IN THE FOLLOWING, *c* OR *g* ENDING A SYLLABLE HAVING *ʌ* PRIMARY OR SECONDARY ACCENT, IS SOUNDED AS *s* AND, RESPECTIVELY.

pub lic′ i ty	ex plic′ it	tac i tur′ ni ty
ra pac′ i ty	so lic′ it	mag is te′ ri al
sa gac′ i ty	im ag′ ine	a troc′ i ty
bel lig′ er ent	au dac′ i ty	fe roc′ i ty
o rig′ i nal	ca pac′ i ty	ve loc′ i ty
ver tig′ i nous	lo quac′ i ty	rhi noc′ e ros
ar mig′ er ous	men dac′ i ty	rec i proc′ i ty
re frig′ er ate	il leg′ i ble	im ag in a′ tion
rec i ta′ tion	o rig′ i nate	ex ag ger a′ tio
veg e ta′ tion	so lic′ i tor	re frig er a′ tion
ag i ta′ tion	fe lic′ i ty	so lic i ta′ tion
cog i ta′ tion	mu nic′ i pal	fe lic i ta′ tion
o le ag′ i nous	an tic′ i pate	leg er de main′

DICTATION.

Too oft we pine at ills unseen,
    And from the future borrow,
And load ourselves till we careen
    With what may be to-morrow.

Thus with a world of care we hedge
    Ourselves, and little know it—
By ever crossing o'er the bridge
    Before we have come to it.
               J. W. HARRINGTON.

LESSON 176.

WORDS IN WHICH *g*, BEFORE *e*, *i* AND *y*, HAS ITS HARD OR
CLOSE SOUND.

gear	lug' ger	clog' ging	gid' dy
geese	snag' ged	clog' gy	gig' gle
gift	snag' gy	bag' gy	gig' gling
give	sprig' gy	dog' ged	gig' gler
gig	stag' ger	dog' gish	gim' let
gild	ea' ger	jogged	girl' ish
gimp	mea' ger	jog' ging	jag' ged
gird	ti' ger	jog' ger	jag' gy
girth	brag' ger	crag' ger	gag' ging
leg' gin	dag' ger	dig' ger	brag' ging
quag' gy	crag' gy	dig' ging	bag' ging

rag' ged	bug' gy	hugged	geld' ing
trig' ger	twig' gy	hug' ging	gild' ing
scrag' ged	wag' gish	shrugged	gild' ed
scrag' gy	wag' ging	shrug' ging	gild' er
shag' gy	au' ger	rug' ged	swag' ger
shag' ged	bog' gy	tugged	swag' gy
slug' gish	fog' gy	tug' ging	gird' le
rig' ging	sog' gy	lug' ging	gird' er
rigged	gib' ber ish	mug' gy	wagged
rig' ger	nog' gin	lugged	wag' ger y
flag' ging	tar' get	fagged	log ger head'
flag' gy	gift' ed	fag' ging	to geth' er

8

LESSON 177.

WORDS IN WHICH c BEFORE h HAS THE SOUND OF k.

chyle	chem' ist	chro nom' e ter
scheme	an' chor	arch' i tect
ache	ech' o	arch' i trave
chasm	chron' ic	arch' e type
chrism	sched' ule	hep' tar chy
chord	pas' chal	mach' i nate
chyme	chol' er	lach' ry mal
school	cho' rist	sac' cha rine
choir	schol' ar	syn' chro nism
chro' mo	mon' arch	chor' is ter
cho' rus	stom' ach	chron' i cle
cho' ral	an' ar chy	or' ches tra

ar' chives	chrys' o lite	pa' tri arch
cha' os	char' ac ter	eu' cha rist
ep' och	cat' e chism	chi me' ra
o' cher	pen' ta teuch	pa ro' chi al
tro' chee	sep' ul cher	cha me' le on
chro mat' ic	tech' nic al	the om' a chy
me chan' ic	syn ec' do che	mel' an chol y
cha ot' ic	mo narch' ic al	pa' tri arch y
scho las' tic	bron chot' o my	hi' er arch y
ca chex' y	chro nol' o gy	ol' i gar chy
cha lyb' e ate	chi rog' ra phy	cat e chet' ic al
a nach' ro nism	cho rog' ra phy	ich' thy ol o gy

LESSON 178.

WORDS IN WHICH THE LETTER *e* STANDS BEFORE *i*.

ceil	de ceive′	leis′ ure	re ceipt′
ceil′ ing	per ceive′	nei′ ther	seine
con ceit′	dis seize′	o bei′ sance	seize
con ceive′	ei′ ther	o bei′ sant	sei′ zin
de ceit′	in vei′ gle	re ceive′	seiz′ ure

WORDS IN WHICH THE LETTER *i* STANDS BEFORE *e*.

a chieve′	fiend	pier	siege
grieve	brig a dier′	pierce	thief
griev′ ance	bre vier′	priest	thieve
griev′ ous	fierce	re lief′	tier
ag grieve′	lief	re lieve′	tierce
be lief′	liege	re prieve′	wield
be lieve′	lien	bom bar dier′	yield
brief	mien	gren a dier′	fin an cier′
chief	niece	can non ier′	cav a lier′
field	piece	re trieve′	chev a lier′

DICTATION.

North Carolina feels that she is one of the elder daughters of the great American family, and in all the higher and sublimer elements of character the equal of any; because she has a record and a history that she is justly proud of, and that cannot be taken away from her either by her enemies or the ephemeral politicians of the hour.—J. M. LEACH.

LESSON 179.

IRREGULAR WORDS.

bra' sier	pro fu' sion	il lu' sion	col lis' ion
gla' zier	ab ra' sion	in fu' sion	de cis' ion
gra' zier	col lu' sion	in va' sion	de ris' ion
ho' sier	con clu' sion	suf fu' sion	e lis' ion
o' sier	con fu' sion	dis sua' sion	pre cis' ion
cro' sier	cor ro' sion	per sua' sion	re vis' ion
fu' sion	oc ca' sion	am bro' sia	re scis' sion
af fu' sion	per va' sion	am bro' sial	con cis' ion
co he' sion	e lu' sion	ob tru' sion	ex cis' ion
ad he' sion	dif fu' sion	de tru' sion	di vis' ion
de lu' sion	dis plo' sion	in tru' sion	in cis' ion

LESSON 180.

com bus' tion	be hav' ior	brill' ian cy	court' ier
in di ges' tion	pe cul' iar	brill' iant ly	cloth' ier
ex haus' tion	fa mil' iar ize	mil' ia ry	bill' iards
sug ges' tion	o pin' ion ist	val' iant ly	mill' ion
com pan' ion	fus' tian	val' iant ness	min' ion
do min' ion	con ges' tion	com mun' ion	pin' ion
o pin' ion	di ges' tion	ver mil' ion	scull' ion
re bell' ion	ad mix' tion	pa vil' ion	trill' ion
re bell' ious	sav' ior	pos till 'ion	trunn' ion
ci vil' ian	jun' ior	fa mil' iar	brill' iant
sen' ior	val' iant	bat tal' ion	fil' ial
bil' ious	on' ion	mix' tion	coll' ier

LESSON 181.

w IS SOUNDED BEFORE h.

whale	white	whiff	whist	whis' key
wheat	whi' ten	whig	whit	whis' ker
wharf	white' wash	whim	whiz	whis' tle
what	whi' tish	whip	where	whith' er
wheel	whi' ting	whelm	whey	whit' low
wheeze	why	whelp	wheth' er	whit' tle
whee' dle	whet	when	whet' stone	whirl
whine	which	whence	whim' per	whirl' pool
while	whilk	whisk	whis' per	wharf' age

IN THE FOLLOWING WORDS w IS SILENT.

who	whole	whole' some	whole' sale
whom	whoop	who so ev' er	who ev' er
whose	whol' ly	whom so ev' er	whoop' ing

LESSON 182.

WORDS OF THREE SYLLABLES, ACCENTED ON THE SECOND.

ac com' plish	as ton' ish	em broid' er	por tent' ous
es tab lish	dis tin guish	re join der	a bun dant
em bel lish	ex tin guish	e nor mous	re dun dant
a bol ish	re lin quish	dis as trous	dis cor dant
re plen ish	ex.cul pate	al li ance	as sail ant
di min ish	con trib ute	re li ance	so no rous
ad mon ish	re mon strance	con sum mate	a ce tous
pre mon ish	tri umph ant	mo ment ous	con ca vous

LESSON 183.

WORDS IN WHICH *th* HAS ITS VOCAL SOUND.

nei′ ther	fur′ thest	fur′ ther	wor′ thy
weth′ er	poth′ er	breth′ ren	moth′ er
bur′ then	ei′ ther	whith′ er	smoth′ er
south′ ern	nei′ ther	wheth′ er	oth′ er
teth′ er	hea′ then	leath′ er	with′ er
thith′ er	cloth′ ier	feath′ er	with draw′
with′ er	rath′ er	there with al′	an oth′ er
lath′ er	fath′ om	nev er the less′	to geth′ er
fa′ ther	gath′ er	weath′ er	the
far′ thing	hith′ er	broth′ er	those
this	thou	blithe	smooth
that	thee	tithe	soothe
thine	them	lithe	they
thy	thence	writhe	there
then	these	scythe	their
thus	than	though	thong

LESSON 184.

WORDS IN WHICH *th* HAS ITS ASPIRATED SOUND.

e′ ther	thim′ ble	ap′ a thy	an tith′ e sis
the′ sis	in thrall′	æs thet′ ics	mis an′ thro py
ze′ nith	a thwart′	syn′ the sis	phi lan′ thro py
thick′ et	be troth′	pan the′ on	the oc′ ra cy
thun′ der	be neath′	e the′ re al	the ol′ o gy
this′ tle	be queath′	ca the′ dral	ther mom′ e ter
thros′ tle	thor′ ough	au then′ tic	my thol′ o gy

LESSON 185.

WORDS IN WHICH *th* HAS ITS ASPIRATED SOUND.

throt' tle	thou' sand	pa thet' ic	or thog' ra phy
thirst' y	a' the ism	syn thet' ic	hy poth' e sis
thrift' y	the' o ry	ath let' ic	li thog' ra phy
threat' en	the' o rem	a the ist' ic	a poth' e ca ry
au' thor	cath' o lic	the o ret' ic al	ap o the' o sis
meth' od	ep' i thet	me thod' ic al	pol' y the ism
an' them	lab' y rinth	math e mat' ics	bib li o the' cal
diph' thong	leth' ar gy	en thu' si asm	ich thy ol' o gy
eth' ics	sym' pa thy	an tip' a thy	or ni thol' o gy
pan' ther	am' a ranth	a rith' me tic	a rith me ti' cian

LESSON 186.

IN THE FOLLOWING WORDS *th* HAS THE ASPIRATED SOUND.

theme	thieve	filth	thin	berth
three	faith	thwack	thank	thwart
thrice	thigh	broth	thick	warmth
throne	throat	cloth	thrill	swath
throw	doth	froth	thumb	path
truth	throe	loth	thump	bath
youth	throve	moth	length	lath
heath	teeth	troth	strength	wrath
ruth	threw	north	hath	hearth
sheath	thrive	sloth	withe	tooth
both	thread	thought	thatch	birth
oath	thresh	thorn	thrill	mirth
quoth	thrift	throb	thrush	thirst

PART II.

WORDS CLASSIFIED ACCORDING TO THEIR
GENERAL USE, AND PROPER NAMES FOUND
IN THE GEOGRAPHY AND HISTORY OF
NORTH CAROLINA.

LESSON 1.

THE FARM AND ITS PRODUCTS.

land	ten' ant	horse	marsh	woods
sta' ble	fence	cart	swamp	yards
barn	rail	axe	stream	hedge
dai' ry	post	hoe	stone	hill
field	for' est	rake	plan ta' tion	dale
home	ground	plow	earth.	val' ley
plan' ter	wag' on	spade	ditch	gar' den
farm' er	ag ri cul' ture	shov' el	creek	fer' tile

LESSON 2.

man' or	spring	hoe' ing	shuck' ing
fer' til i zer	bar' ren	weed' ing	drain' ing
marl	sand' y	till' ing	wa' ter ing
gu a' no	bog' gy	mow' ing	dig' ging
phos' phate	rock' y	reap' ing	maul' ing
mead' ow	saw	bind' ing	spad' ing
pas' ture	fruit' ful	haul' ing	feed' ing
low' land	plow' ing	seed' ing	milk' ing
up' land	plant' ing	husk' ing	chop' ping
drain	sow' ing	ditch' ing	fenc' ing

LESSON 3.

shell' er	thresh' er	scythe	sick' le
reap' er	sheaf	har' row	mow' er
cra' dle	wheat	rye	cab' bage
crop	corn	po ta' to	bar' ley
grain	oats	tur' nip	grass
clo' ver	flax	tim' o thy	mil' let
straw	hay	fod' der	shuck
cot' ton	ap' ple	pear	peach
to bac' co	rad' ish	plum	prune
hemp	col' lard	straw' ber ry	rasp' ber ry

LESSON 4.

quince	a' pri cot	cher' ry	or' ange
cit' ron	lem' on	ol' ive	grape
beet	on' ion	leak	spin' ach
as par' a gus	o' kra	gar' lic	to ma' to
pars' nip	squash	cym' ling	gourd
pump' kin	can' ta loupe	wa' ter mel on	peas
let' tuce	bean	cu' cum ber	mul' ber ry
cel' e ry	rhu' barb	pep' per	dew' ber ry
pars' ley	mus' tard	cran' ber ry	ber' ries
car' rot	cur' rant	sage	thyme

LESSON 5.

MERCANTILE TERMS.

mer′ chant	buy′ er	cus′ tom er	debt′ or
cred′ it or	ac count′	mon′ ey	spe′ cie
prof′ it	pur′ chase	de pos′ it	dis′ count
draft	note	ac cept′ ance	sol′ vent
cur′ ren cy	treas′ u ry	bank	ex change′
fail	gain	loss	bar′ ter
trade	or′ der	u′ su ry	in′ ter est
for ge′ ry	def′ i cit	bank′ rupt	no′ ta ry
as sign′ ment	cash ier′	tel′ ler	di rect′ ors
book′ keep er	spec′ u late	sig′ na ture	cap′ i tal
ap prais′ al	ad vi′ ces	con′ sign ee	cop′ y right

LESSON 6.

mort′ gage	check	pound	ounce
in′ voice	clerk	store	stock
fin an cier′	auc tion eer′	de liv′ er y	em po′ ri um
in′ ven to ry	in dors′ er	em bez′ zle	mill′ ion aire
sales′ man	se cu′ ri ty	pre′ mi um	pol′ i cy
com′ merce	con′ tract	part′ ner ship	pay′ ment
ware′ house	a′ gent	part′ ner	bal′ ance
in solv′ ent	bank′ er	bro′ ker	clear′ ance
in sure′	deal′ er	dol′ lar	rich′ es
vo ca′ tion	traf′ fic	cent	ex tor′ tion
in dem′ ni ty	gaug′ ing	fore clos′ ure	cou′ pon

LESSON 7.

sus pen' sion	par	buy	sell
pro' ceeds	of' fice	freight	coin
wa' ges	spend' thrift	ex press'	re ceipt'
mark' er	a mount'	mail	col lec' tion
port' er	bar' gain	post' age	no' tions
as sign'	shil' ling	bull' ion	thrift' y
ar rears'	in' come	vend' er	ad' ver tise
de fault'	tar' iff	type' wri ter	mar' ket
ex pense'	stor' age	way' bill	com mis' sion
trans act'	wharf' age	ship' ping	drum' mer
no' ta ry	pro' test	quar' an tine	ton' nage
at tach' ment	rev' e nue	re sour' ces	ma tu' ri ty

LESSON 8.

NAMES OF FLOWERS.

dai' sy	nar cis' sus	lil' y	co' le us
cac' tus	gla di' o lus	a za' le a	pan' sy
mign on ette'	gen' tian	lav' en der	cro' cus
fuch' si a	cal' la	a em' o ne	pe' o ny
ge ra' ni um	tube' rose	or' chis	pop' py
mar' i gold	ox a' lis	sy rin' ga	pink
crys an' the mum	dan' de li on	rho do den' dron	clem' a tis
vi' o let	car na' tion	pe tu' ria	ar bu' tus
prim' rose	daf' fo dil	ca mel' li a	blue' bell
ai lan' tus	tu' lip	sun flow' er	myr' tle
ver be' na	snow' drop	he' li o trope	o le an' der
li' lac	jon' quil	hy' a cinth	mag no' lia

LESSON 9.

BIRDS AND ANIMALS.

ea′ gle	swan	duck	plov′ er
goose	cuck′ oo	lark	chick′ en
gan′ der	roost′ er	pe′ trel	part′ ridge
mock′ ing bird	pig′ eon	pul′ let	gull
buz′ zard	blue′ bird	hawk	hen
tom′ tit	black′ bird	snipe	spar′ row
wood′ cock	thrush	wren	her′ on
crow	swal′ low	bat	rob′ in
star′ ling	pea′ fowl	o′ ri ole	sky′ lark
rice′ bird	tur′ key	guin′ ea fowl	crane

LESSON 10.

king′ fish er	jay	dove	cam′ el
jack′ daw	owl	whip′ poor will	heif′ er
horse	dog	cat	marsh′ hen
mouse	deer	ox	rat
squir′ rel	rab′ bit	bear	cow
bull	goat	sheep	wolf
leop′ ard	lamb	mon′ key	li′ on
ti′ ger	pan′ ther	hy′ e na	rac′ coon
o pos′ sum	kit′ ten	lynx	ot′ ter
musk′ rat	fer′ ret	ground′ hog	wea′ sel

LESSON 11.

el' e phant	dor' mouse	bab' oon	jag' uar
gi raffe'	go ril' la	mus' tang	jack' all
mas' tiff	mar' mot	span' iel	po' ny
point' er	ga zelle'	por' cu pine	an' te lope
ter' rier	kang' a roo	gua na' co	sa' ble
ta' pir	cat' a mount	bea' ver	lla' ma
wal' rus	buf' fa lo	gnu	badg' er
bi' son	elk	rhi noc' e ros	ape
cham' ois	chim pan' zee	o rang' ou tang'	al pac' a
drom' e da ry	hip po pot' a mus	ze' bra	i' bex

LESSON 12.

THE BODY.

head	skin	wind' pipe	lungs	wrist
hair	veins	pal' ate	heart	thumb
scalp	palm	breast	stom' ach	thigh
eye	groin	nerves	liv' er	leg
eye' lash	tooth	blood	shoul' der	knee
eye' lid	mouth	ar' ter ies	hand	an' kle
eye' ball	nose	lar' ynx	nails	foot
eye' brow	nos' tril	back	mus' cles	toes
skull	cheek	chest	trunk	joint
fore' head	tongue	waist	brain	bones
ear	throat	hip	arm	ten' dons
pu' pil	neck	spine	fin' ger	in' step
flesh	chin	ribs	el' bow	mar' row
heel	gums	spleen	bow' els	sin' ew

LESSON 13.

DISEASES.

mumps	scrof′ u la	dys en ter′ y	ty phoid′
hys ter′ ics	small′ pox	di ar rhœ′ a	tu′ mor
car′ bun cle	pneu mo′ ni a	mea′ sles	asth′ ma
bron chi′ tis	hy dro pho′ bi a	drop′ sy	nerv′ ous
bun′ ion	lar′ yn gi tis	head′ ache	cough
boil	ep′ i lep sy	ear′ ache	nau′ se a
corn	va′ ri o loid	hic′ cough	chol′ er a
wart	pa ral′ y sis	rheu′ ma tism	pleu′ ri sy
croup	ep i lep′ tic	e ry sip′ e las	lu′ na cy
a′ gue	neu ral′ gi a	con sump′ tion	whoop′ ing
fe′ ver	ca tarrh′	con ges′ tion	chil′ blain
ty′ phus	scar la ti′ na	diph the′ ri a	gan′ grene
ver′ ti go	ap′ o plex y	tooth′ ache	ma′ ni a
de lir′ i um	dys pep′ si a	can′ cer	men in gi′ ti

LESSON 14.

ORDINALS.

first	ninth	sev′ en teenth	sev′ en ti eth
sec′ ond	tenth	eight′ eenth	eight′ i eth
third	e lev′ enth	nine′ teenth	nine′ ti eth
fourth	twelfth	twen′ ti eth	hun′ dredth
fifth	thir′ teenth	thir′ ti eth	thou′ sandth
sixth	four′ teenth	for′ ti eth	mill′ ionth
sev′ enth	fif′ teenth	fif′ ti eth	bill′ ionth
eighth	six′ teenth	six′ ti eth	quad′ rill iont

LESSON 15.

NUMERALS.

ɔne	nine	sev' eu teen	sev' en ty
wo	ten	eight' een	eight' y
hree	e lev' en	niue' teen	nine' ty
ɔur	twelve	twen' ty	hun dred
ive	thir' teen	thir' ty	thou' sand
ix	four' teen	for' ty	mill' ion
ev' en	fif' teen	fif' ty	bill' ion
ight	six' teen	six' ty	quad' rill ion

LESSON 16.

NAMES OF THE MONTHS AND DAYS.

an' u a ry	Ju ly'	Mon' day	Sun' day
ʼeb' ru a ry	Au' gust	Tues' day	Christ' mas
ʃarch	Sep tem' ber	Wednes' day	East' er
ʌpril	Oc to' ber	Thurs' day	Thanks' giv ing
ʃay	No vem' ber	Fri' day	In de pend' ence
une	De cem' ber	Sat' ur day	Me mo' ri al

LESSON 17.

NAMES OF THE STATES OF THE UNION.

Al a ba' ma	Maine	O hi' o
Ar kan' sas	Ma' ry land	Or' e gon
Cal i for' ni a	Mass a chu' setts	Penn syl va' ni a
Col o ra' do	Mich' i gan	Rhode Is' land
Con nec' ti cut	Min ne so' ta	South Car o li' na
Del' a ware	Mis sis sip' pi	South Da ko' ta
Flor' i da	Mis sou' ri	Tenn es see'
Geor' gi a	Mon ta' na	Tex' as
I' da ho	Ne bras' ka	Ver mont'
Ill i nois'	Ne va' da	Vir gin' i a
I o' wa	New Jer' sey	Wash' ing ton
In di an' a	New Hamp' shire	West Vir gin' i a
Kan' sas	New York	Wis con' sin
Ken tuck' y	North Car o li' na	Wy' o ming
Lou is i an' a	North Da ko' ta	

TERRITORIES.

A las' ka	In' di an	Ok la ho' ma
Ar i zo' na	New Mex' i co	U' tah

LESSON 18.

PRESIDENTS OF THE UNITED STATES.

1 George Washington
2 John Adams
3 Thomas Jefferson
4 James Madison
5 James Monroe
6 John Quincy Adams
7 Andrew Jackson
8 Martin Van Buren
9 William Henry Harrison
0 John Tyler
1 James Knox Polk

12 Zachary Taylor
13 Millard Fillmore
14 Franklin Pierce
15 James Buchanan
16 Abraham Lincoln
17 Andrew Johnson
18 Ulysses Simpson Grant
19 Rutherford Burchard Hayes
20 James Abram Garfield
21 Chester Alan Arthur
22 Grover Cleveland

23 Benjamin Harrison

LESSON 19.

CHRISTIAN NAMES OF MEN.

Ab' ner	A' mos	Ben' e dict	Claude
Ad' am	An' drew	Ben' ja min	Con' rad
A dol' phus	An' tho ny	Ber' nard	Cor ne' li us
Al' an	Arch' i bald	Cæ' sar	Cy' rus
Al' bert	Ar' nold	Ca' leb	Dan' iel
Al ex an' der	Ar' thur	Cal' vin	Da' vid
Al' fred	Aus' tin	Ce' cil	Den' nis
A lon' zo	Au gus' tus	Charles	Don' ald
Al phon' so	Bar thol' o mew	Chris' to pher	Dun' can
Am' brose	Bas' il	Clar' ence	E' ben

9

LESSON 20.

CHRISTIAN NAMES OF MEN.

Ed' mund	Eus' tace	Gil' bert	Hugh
Ed' ward	Ev' er ard	God' win	I' saac
Ed' win	Fer' di nand	Greg' o ry	I' van
Eg' bert	Fran' cis	Guy	I sa' i ah
E li' as	Frank	Har' old	Ja' cob
E li' jah	Frank' lin	Hen' ry	James
E li' sha	Fred' er ick	Her' bert	Jas' per
E ras' tus	Geof' frey	Her' mon	Je rome'
Er' nest	George	Hor' ace	Jes' se
Eu gene'	Ger' ald	Hu' bert	John

———

LESSON 21.

Jon' a than	Le' o pold	Mar cil' lus	Na than' i el
Jo' seph	Lew' is	Mark	Neal
Josh' u a	Li' o nel	Mar' tin	Nor' man
Ju' li an	Lo ren' zo	Mar' ma duke	Oc ta' vi us
Ju' li us	Lou' is	Mat' thew	Ol' i ver
Ken' neth	Lu' ci an	Mau' rice	Or lan' do
Lam' bert	Lu' ci us	Mi' cha el	Os' car
Law' rence	Luke	Miles	Os' wald
Leon' ard	Lu' ther	Mo' ses	O' wen
Le on' i das	Ly cur' gus	Na' than	Pat' rick

LESSON 22.

CHRISTIAN NAMES OF MEN.

Paul	Rod' er ick	Si' mon	U' lys ses
Pe' ter	Ru' dolph	Sol' o mon	Vic' tor
Phil' ip	Row' land	Ste' phen	Vin' cent
Ralph	Ru' fus	Syl' ves ter	Wal' ter
Ray' mond	Sam' u el	Thad' de us	Wil' liam
Reg' i nald	Se' bas ti an	The' o dore	Win' fred
Reu' ben	Seth	The oph' i lus	Zach a ri' ah
Reyn' old	Si' las	Thom' as	Zach' a ry
Rich' ard	Sil va' nus	Tim' o thy	Zeb' e dee
Rob' ert	Sim' e on	Ti' tus	Zeb' u lon

LESSON 23.

CHRISTIAN NAMES OF WOMEN.

A' da	A' my	Brid' get	Clau' di a
Ad' a line	An' na	Ca mil' la	Con' stance
Ad' e laide	An toi nette'	Car o li' na	Cor de' li a
Ag' a tha	Ar a bel' la	Cath' a rine	Co rin' na
Ag' nes	Au gus' ta	Cec' i ly	Cor ne' li a
Al ber' ta	Au re' li a	Ce' lia	Cyn' thi a
Al' ice	Au ro' ra	Char' lotte	De' li a
Al mi' ra	Bar' ba ra	Chlo' e	Di an' a
A man' da	Be' a trice	Chris ti' na	Di' nah
Am' a bel	Ber' tha	Clar' a	Dor' o thy
A me' lia	Blanche	Cla ris' sa	E' dith

LESSON 24.

CHRISTIAN NAMES OF WOMEN.

Ed' na	Eu ge' ni a	Flo' ra	Har' ri et
El' e a nor	Eu la' li a	Flor' ence	Hel' e na
E liz' a beth	Eu' nice	Fran' ces	Hen ri et' ta
E li' za	E' va	Fred er i' ca	Hes' ter
El vi' ra	E van' ge line	Geor gi an' a	Hope
Em' e line	Ev e li' na	Ger' al dine	Ho no' ri a
Em' i ly	Ev' e line	Ger' trude	Hor ten' si a
Em' ma	Fan' ny	Grace	Hul' dah
Es' ther	Fe li' ci a	Gra' tia	I' da
Eu do' ra	Fi de' li a	Han' nah	I' nez

LESSON 25.

I rene'	Ju' li a	Lo rin' da	Mar' tha
Is' a bel	Ju li an' a	Lou i' sa	Ma' ry
Is a bel' la	Ju' li et	Lou ise'	Ma til' da
Jane	Jus ti' na	Lu cin' da	Maud
Ja net'	Kath' a rine	Lu cre' tia	Me hit' a ble
Jean	Lau' ra	Lyd' ia	Me lis' sa
Jean nette'	La vin' i a	Ma' bel	Mil' dred
Joan	Le o no' ra	Mad' e line	Mir' i am
Jo se' pha	Le ti' ti a	Mar' ci a	My' ra
Jo' seph ine	Lil' i an	Mar' ga ret	Oc ta' vi a
Ju' dith	Lil' ly	Ma ri' a	Ol' ive

LESSON 26.

CHRISTIAN NAMES OF WOMEN.

O liv' i a	Re bec' ca	Sa' ra	The o do' si a
O phe' li a	Rho' da	Se li' na	The re' sa
Pau li' na	Ro' sa	Se re' na	Ur' su la
Pau line'	Ros' a bel	Sib' yl	Va le' ri a
Pe nel' o pe	Ros' a lie	So phi' a	Vic to' ri a
Phe' be	Ros' a lind	So phro' ni a	Vi o' la
Phi lip' pa	Ros' a mond	Stel' la	Vir gin' i a
Phyl' lis	Rox an' a	Su' san	Viv' i an
Phœ' be	Ruth	Su san' nah	Win' i fred
Pris cil' la	Sa lome'	Ta bi' tha	Ze no' bi a
Ra' chel	Sa' rah	The o do' ra	

LESSON 27.

CONTRACTIONS AND DIMINUTIVES OF PROPER NAMES.

Alex	Dan	Jim' my	Per' ry
Arch	Dave	Jer' ry	Ralph
Gus	Do' ra	Jack	Rube
Buck	Ed' die	Joe	Dick
Bart	Man' ny	Jule	Bob
Ben	Ras' tus	Lau' ry	Bob' bie
Ben' nie	Ford	Matt	Sam
Char' lie	Frank	Mike	Sebe
Chris	Fred	Nat	Steve
Clem	Har' ry	Nick	Thad

LESSON 28.

CONTRACTIONS AND DIMINUTIONS OF PROPER NAMES.

Ne′ cy	Jake	Pat	Tom
Tom′ mie	Man′ dy	Ka′ tie	El′ len
Tim	Net′ ty	Cis	Hel′ en
Tobe	Belle	Lot′ tie	El′ la
To′ by	Bel′ la	Lot′ ta	No′ ra
Vic	Re′ lia	Clare	Nell
Bill	Bet′ sy	Claud	Bet′ tie
Bil′ lie	Bet′ tie	Co′ ra	Bess
Wil′ lie	Bid′ dy	Nel′ ie	Ef′ fie
Zach	Car′ rie	Deb′ by	Ef′ fa
Ad′ die	Cad′ die	Die	Fan′ ny

LESSON 29.

Ber′ ta	Kate	Dol′ ly	Fan′ nie
Ger′ tie	Lou′ lie	Pat′ sy	Ta′ vy
Gris′ sie	Lou	Pat′ ty	Beck′ y
Hat′ tie	Lu′ cy	Moll	Sal′ ly
Nel′ ly	Maud	Mol′ lie	So′ phy
Et′ ta	Meg	Pol	Su′ sie
Het′ ty	Mag′ gie	Pol′ ly	Su′ ky
Phe′ ny	Peg′ gy	May	Sue
Jo′ sy	Mar′ gie	Mi′ na	Do′ ra
Ju′ dy	Me′ ta	Ni′ na	Ter′ ry
Ju′ lie	Mat	Nan	Tra′ cy
Lil′ lie	Mat′ tie	To′ ny	Wil′ mot

LESSON 30.

FAMILIAR COMPOUND WORDS.

To be always written with a hyphen.

horse-rad ish
high-press ure
bal ance-wheel
mince-pie
safe ty-valve
writ ing-books
pa per-weight
seal ing-wax
bass-viol
blot ting-pa per

tis sue-pa per
trip-ham mer
store-house
sky-light
head-rest
wa ter-color
oil-col or
dress-maker
post-of fice
bond-hol der

grape-shot
lat tice-win dow
light-house
snow-drop
live-oak
dog-wood
rose-wood
dew-ber ry
post-mark
book-keep er

LESSON 31.

bay-win dow
Gulf-stream
pole-star
for get-me-not
white-oak
box-wood
ar bor-vi tæ
morn ing-glo ry
un der-grad u ate
sem i-an nu al

re-as sert
re-ap point
sem i-month ly
half-hol i day
all-hail
jack-o-lant ern
bed-bug
whip-poor-will
half-pay
half-broth er

half-sis ter
half-mast
semi-colon
fair y-like
blow-pipe
bum ble-bee
boa-con strict or
night-hawk
ant-eat er
o rang-ou tang

LESSON 32.

FAMILIAR COMPOUND WORDS.

hum ming-bird	leap-year	sand-pa per
yel low-bird	dog-days	crow-bar
sum mer-time	cut-throat	jack-plane
to-day	foot-pad	steam-en gine
to-mor row	tread-mill	worn-out
house-keep er	chief-just ice	check-rein
ring-lead er	pen-rack	air-pump
draw-bridge	arm-rest	book-shelves
musk-rat	show-card	fortune-tell er
house-fly	hair-cut ter	wood-house
horse-fly	sweet-oil	dress ing-room

LESSON 33.

hair-oil	work-bench	hard-tack
ice-cream	cot ton-gin	su gar-bowl
salt-cel lar	cot ton-press	fire-place
water-mel on	wa ter ing-pot	pure-mind ed
musk-mel on	ring-worm	well-be haved
well-dressed	foot-ball	short-cake
pen-hold er	base-ball	foot-stool
job-work	May-day	tooth-pick
show-bill	New-year	spell ing-book
cas tor-oil	tooth-brush	air-tight
calf-skin	tow el-stand	base-burn er

LESSON 34.

FAMILIAR COMPOUND WORDS.

bill-head
cash-boy
cat-boat
cold-blood ed
co-op er a tive
corn-shuck
cross-ref er ence
des sert-spoon
dress-goods
drive-a way
field-glass

flea-bit ten
four-in-hand
gang-plow
hat-stand
but ton-hole
fog-horn
air-brake
back-set tler
bak ing-pow der
bread-win ner
bric-a-brac

Christ mas-tree
cook-book
corn-cob
corn-field
school-teach er
door-post
drop-light
ear-ring
fash ion-plate
fog-horn
free-trade

LESSON 35.

hay-fe ver
health-lift
herd-book
hur dle-race
ket tle-drum
lawn-ten nis
light-ship
mad-stone
milk-sick
mound-build er
mu sic-box

neck-wear
book-store
oil-mill
om ni bus-bill
or der-book
oys ter-bed
pal ace-car
pen-wip er
pil low-sham
boot-jack
post al-card

race-track
hose-com pa ny
jig-saw
lap-board
let ter-book
low-necked
make-up
pen sion-bill
mouth-or gan
na vy-yard
news-stand

LESSON 36.

FAMILIAR COMPOUND WORDS.

ob ject-les son
oil-well
one-horse
o ver-lap
paint-box
pass-book
pict ure-book
pi lot-boat
pipe-clay
praise-meet ing
re-ar range

re-com mence
rock-can dy
sail-boat
school-board
sea-lev el
sev en-shoot er
shop-worn
sight-draft
spell ing-match
spend ing-mon ey
stem-wind er

street-car
tale-bear er
time-lock
trade-dol lar
type-wri ter
vis it ing-card
wall-tent
wa ter-ice
weath er-bu reau
ring-mas ter
roll er-skate

LESSON 37.

sand-stone
school-ship
sem i-an gle
sheep-dog
back-num ber
smok ing-car
spell ing-bee
stage-whis per
store-clothes
trench-plow
ten-strike

tow-head
tram-way
un der-ground
vice-con sul
wall-flow er
wa ter-fall
wax-plant
weath er-re port
wheel-plow
wine-bib ber
yacht-club

yeast-pow der
high-mind ed
ea gle-eyed
wa ter-tow er
wild-fire
work ing-man
yan kee-doo dle
left-hand ed
free-pass
Sun day-school
sand-fid dler

GOVERNORS OF NORTH CAROLINA.

LESSON 38.

UNDER THE LORDS PROPRIETORS.

1 William Drummond
2 Samuel Stephens
3 George Carteret
4 Thomas Eastchurch
5 Thomas Miller
6 John Harvey
7 John Jenkins
8 Henry Wilkinson
9 Seth Sothel
0 Philip Ludwell
1 Alexander Lillington
12 Thomas Harvey
13 Henderson Walker
14 Robert Daniel
15 Thomas Carey
16 William Glover
17 Edward Hyde
18 Thomas Pollok
19 Charles Eden
20 William Reid
21 George Burrington
22 Richard Everard

ROYAL GOVERNORS.

George Burrington
Nathaniel Rice
Gabriel Johnston
Matthew Rowan
5 Arthur Dobbs
6 William Tryon
7 James Hasell
8 Josiah Martin

North Carolina declared its independence of English government at Charlotte, Mecklenburg county, on the 20th of

LESSON 39.

GOVERNORS UNDER THE CONSTITUTION OF 1776.

1	Richard Caswell	13	David Stone
2	Abner Nash	14	Benjamin Smith
3	Thomas Burke	15	William Hawkins
4	Alexander Martin	16	William Miller
5	Samuel Johnston	17	John Branch
6	Richard Dobbs Spaight	18	Jesse Franklin
7	Samuel Ashe	19	Gabriel Holmes
8	William Richardson Davie	20	Hutchins G. Brown
9	Benjamin Williams	21	James Iredell
10	John Baptiste Ashe	22	John Owen
11	James Turner	23	Montford Stokes
12	Nathaniel Alexander	24	David Lowry Swain

25 Richard Dobbs Spaight, Jr.

LESSON 40.

GOVERNORS ELECTED BY THE PEOPLE.

1	Edward B. Dudley	10	Zebulon B. Vance
2	John M. Morehead	11	William W. Holden
3	William A. Graham	12	Jonathan Worth
4	Charles Manly	13	Tod R. Caldwell
5	David S. Reid	14	Curtis H. Brogden
6	Warren Winslow	15	Thomas J. Jarvis
7	Thomas Bragg	16	Alfred M. Scales
8	John W. Ellis	17	Daniel G. Fowle
9	Henry T. Clark	18	Thomas M. Holt

COUNTIES OF NORTH CAROLINA.

Spell the name of County and tell its origin.

LESSON 41.

County.	Origin of Name.
l′ a mance,	Alamance Creek.
l ex an′ der,	The Alexander family of Mecklenburg county.
l′ le gha ny,	Alleghany Mountains.
n′ son,	Admiral Anson of British Navy.
she,	Governor Samuel Ashe.
eau′ fort,	Henry Somerset, Duke of Beaufort.
er tie′,	James John Bertie, Lords Proprietor.
la′ den,	Martin Bladen.
runs′ wick,	Prince of Brunswick.
un′ combe,	Colonel Edward Buncombe.
urke,	Edmund Burke.

LESSON 42.

a bar′ rus,	Stephen Cabarrus.
ald well′,	Dr. Joseph Caldwell.
am′ den,	Earl of Camden.
ar′ ter et,	Sir George Carteret.
as′ well,	Governor Richard Caswell.
a taw′ ba,	Indian tribe.
hat′ ham,	William Pitt, Earl of Chatham.
her o kee′,	Indian tribe.
how an′,	Indian tribe.
lay,	Henry Clay.
leve′ land,	Colonel Benjamin Cleveland.

LESSON 43.

County.	Origin of Name.
Co lum' bus,	Christopher Columbus.
Cra' ven,	William, Earl of Craven.
Cum' ber land,	Duke of Cumberland.
Cur ri tuck',	Indian tribe.
Dare,	Virginia Dare.
Da' vid son,	General William Davidson.
Da' vie,	Governor William R. Davie.
Du' plin,	Lord Duplin.
Dur' ham,	Durham family of that county.
Edge' combe,	Earl of Mount Edgecombe.
For syth',	Colonel Benjamin Forsyth.
Frank' lin,	Benjamin Franklin.

LESSON 44.

Gas' ton,	Judge William Gaston.
Gates,	General Horatio Gates.
Gra' ham,	Governor William A. Graham.
Gran' ville,	John, Earl of Granville.
Greene,	General Nathaniel Greene.
Guil' ford,	Lord North, Earl of Guilford.
Hal' i fax,	Earl of Halifax.
Har' nett,	Cornelius Harnett.
Hay' wood,	Hon. John Haywood, State Treasurer.
Hen' der son,	Judge Leonard Henderson.
Hert' ford,	Marquis of Hertford.
Hyde,	Governor Edward Hyde.
Ire' dell,	Judge James Iredell.

LESSON 45.

County.	Origin of Name.
Jack' son,	General Andrew Jackson.
John' ston,	Governor Gabriel Johnston.
Jones,	General Willie Jones.
Le noir',	General William Lenoir.
Lin' coln,	General Benjamin Lincoln.
Ma' con,	Hon. Nathaniel Macon.
Mad' i son,	President James Madison.
Mar' tin,	Governor Josiah Martin.
Mc Dow' ell,	Colonel Joseph A. McDowell.
Meck' len burg,	Princess Charlotte, of Mecklenburg.
Mitch' ell,	Dr. Elisha Mitchell.
Mont gom' er y,	General Richard Montgomery.

LESSON 46.

Moore,	Judge Alfred Moore.
Nash,	General Francis Nash.
New Han' o ver,	The House of Hanover.
North amp' ton,	George, Earl of Northampton.
Ons' low,	Arthur Onslow.
Or' ange,	The House of Orange.
Pam' li co,	Pamlico River and Sound.
Pas quo tank',	Indian tribe.
Pen' der,	General William Pender.
Per quim' ans,	Indian tribe.
Per' son,	General Thomas Person.
Pitt,	William Pitt, Earl of Chatham.
Polk,	General William Polk.

LESSON 47.

County.	Origin of Name.
Ran' dolph,	Randolph family of Virginia.
Rich' mond,	Duke of Richmond.
Rob' e son,	Colonel Robeson.
Rock' ing ham,	Chas. Watson Wentworth, Marquis of Rock ingham.
Row an',	Governor Matthew Rowan.
Ruth' er ford,	General Griffith Rutherford.
Samp' son,	Colonel John Sampson.
Stan' ly,	Hon. John Stanly.
Stokes,	Hon. John Stokes.
Sur' ry,	Surry County in England.
Swain,	Governor David L. Swain.

LESSON 48.

Tran syl va' nia,	Signifies "Beyond the Woods."
Tyr' rell,	Sir John Tyrrell.
Un' ion,	Union of parts of Anson and Mecklenburg
Vance,	Governor Zebulon B. Vance.
Wake,	Miss Esther Wake.
War' ren,	General Joseph Warren.
Wash' ing ton,	President George Washington.
Wa tau' ga,	Watauga River.
Wayne,	General Anthony Wayne.
Wilkes,	John Wilkes, English Statesman.
Wil' son,	General Louis D. Wilson.
Yad' kin,	Yadkin River.
Yan' cey,	Hon. Bartlett Yancey.

COUNTY TOWNS.

Spell the name of Town and tell where situated.

LESSON 49.

Name of Town.			*In County Situated.*
Ashe' ville,	.	.	Buncombe.
Ash' bo ro,	.	.	Randolph.
Al be marle',	.	.	Stanly.
Beau' fort,	.	.	Carteret.
Ba' kers ville,	.	.	Mitchell.
Bay' bo ro,	.	.	Pamlico.
Bur' gaw,	.	.	Pender.
Bry' son Cit y,	.	.	Swain.
Bre vard',	.	.	Transylvania.
Boone,	.	.	Watauga.
Burns' ville,	.	.	Yancey.

LESSON 50.

Cam' den,	.	.	Camden.
Con' cord,	.	.	Cabarrus.
Cur ri tuck',	.	.	Currituck.
Char' lotte,	.	.	Mecklenburg.
Car' thage,	.	.	Moore.
Co lum' bus,	.	.	Polk.
Clin' ton,	.	.	Sampson.
Co lum' bi a,	.		Tyrrell.
Dur' ham,	.	.	Durham.
Dal' las,	.		Gaston.
Dan' bu ry,	.		Stokes.

10

LESSON 51.

Name of Town.			*In County Situated.*
Dob' son,	.	.	Surry.
E liz' a beth town,		.	Bladen.
E' den ton,	.	.	Chowan.
E liz' a beth City,		.	Pasquotank.
Fay' ette ville,	.	.	Cumberland.
Frank' lin,	.	.	Macon.
Gra' ham,	.	.	Alamance.
Gates' ville,	.	.	Gates.
Greens' bo ro,	.	.	Guilford.
Green' ville,	.	.	Pitt.
Golds' bo ro,	.	.	Wayne.
Hayes' ville,	.	.	Clay.

LESSON 52.

Hal' i fax,	.	.	Halifax.
Hen' der son ville,		.	Henderson.
Hills' bo ro,	.	.	Orange.
Hert' ford,	.	.	Perquimans.
Hen' der son,	.	.	Vance.
Jef' fer son,	.	.	Ashe.
Jack' son,	.	.	Northampton.
Jack' son ville,	.	.	Onslow.
Ke' nans ville,	.	.	Duplin.
Kin' ston,	.	.	Lenoir.
Le noir',	.	.	Caldwell.
Lex' ing ton,	.	.	Davidson.

LESSON 53.

Name of Town.			In County Situated.
Lou' is burg,	.	.	Franklin.
Lil' ling ton,	.	.	Harnett.
Lin' coln ton,	.	.	Lincoln.
Lum' ber ton,	.	.	Robeson.
Mor' gan ton,	.	.	Burke.
Mur' phy,	.	.	Cherokee.
Man' te o,	.	.	Dare.
Mocks' ville,	.	.	Davie.
Mar' shall,	.	.	Madison.
Ma' ri on,	.	.	McDowell.
Mon roe',	.	.	Union.
New' ton,	.	.	Catawba.

LESSON 54.

New' Bern,	.	.	Craven.
Nash' ville,	.	.	Nash.
Ox' ford,	.	.	Granville.
Pitts' bo ro,	.	.	Chatham.
Ply' mouth,	.	.	Washington.
Rob' bins ville,	.	.	Graham.
Rox' bo ro,	.	.	Person.
Rock' ing ham,	.	.	Richmond.
Ruth' er ford ton,		.	Rutherford.
Ral' eigh,	.	.	Wake.
Spar' ta,	.	.	Alleghany.
South' port,	.	.	Brunswick.
Shel' by,	.	.	Cleveland.

LESSON 55.

Name of Town.			In County Situated.
Snow Hill',	.	.	Greene.
Swan Quar' ter,	.	.	Hyde.
States' ville,	.	.	Iredell.
Smith' field,	.	.	Johnston.
Salis' bu ry,	.	.	Rowan.
Tay' lors ville,	.	.	Alexander.
Tar' bo ro,	.	.	Edgecombe.
Tren' ton,	.	.	Jones.
Troy,	.	.	Montgomery.
Wades' bo ro,	.	.	Anson.
Wash' ing ton,	.	.	Beaufort.
Wind' sor,	.	.	Bertie.

LESSON 56.

White' ville,	.	.	Columbus.
Win' ston,	.	.	Forsyth.
Waynes' ville,	.	.	Haywood.
Win' ton,	.	.	Hertford.
Web' ster,	.	.	Jackson.
Wil' liam ston,	.	.	Martin.
Wil' ming ton,	.	.	New Hanover.
Went' worth,	.	.	Rockingham.
War' ren ton,	.	.	Warren.
Wilkes' bo ro,	.	.	Wilkes.
Wil' son,	.	.	Wilson.
Yan' cey ville,	.	.	Caswell.
Yad' kin ville,	.	.	Yadkin.

TOWNS AND VILLAGES IN NORTH CAROLINA.

LESSON 57.

An' son ville
Bat' tle bo ro
Ben' son
Bla' den bo ro
Boone' ville
Bre vard'
Bur' ling ton
Ca' ry
Chad' bourn
Chap el Hill'
Clark' ton
Clay' ton

Clyde
Dunn
Elm Cit' y
El' kin
En' field
Fai' son
Farm' ing ton
Frank' lin ton
Frank' lins ville
Gar' ner
Ga' rys burg
Gas' ton

Gas to' ni a
Gib' son ville
Globe
Gulf
Ham' il ton
Ham' let
Hamp' ton ville
Har' lowe
Har' rells ville
Hick' o ry
High' lands
High Point'

LESSON 58.

Hun' ters ville
James' ville
Jones' bo ro
Ker' ners ville
Key' ser
Kit' trell
LaGrange
Lau' rin burg
Leaks' ville
Leas' burg
Lew' is ton
Liles' ville
O' lin

Lit' tle ton
Ma' con
Mad' i son
Mag no' li a
Man' son
Max' ton
Meb' ane
Mid' dle burg
Mid' dle town
Mil' ton
Moores' bo ro
Moores' ville
Pot e ca' si

More' head Cit y
Mor' ris ville
Mount Air' y
Mur' frees bo ro
Nan ta ha la'
Neuse
New Hill'
New' port
Nor' wood
Oaks
O' cra coke
Old Fort
Rock y Point'

LESSON 59.

Os' good	Prince' ton	Rock y Mount
Paint' er	Ran' dle man	Roles' ville
Pol' loks ville	Reids' ville	Rox' o bel
Pa cif' ic	Rid' dicks ville	Sa' lem
Pal my' ra	Ridge' way	Sa lu' da
Pam' li co	Ridge' ville	San' ford
Pan te' go	Ring' wood	Sax' a pa haw
Pe' kin	Rob' er son ville	Scot land Neck'
Pike' ville	Rob' er dell	Sea' board
Pine' ville	Rob' e son	Sel' ma
Polk' ton	Rob' bins ville	Shal' lotte
Slades' ville	Tay' lors ville	Wax' haw
South ern Pines'	Teach' ey	Wel' don

LESSON 60.

Spar' ta	Thom' as ville	Whit' a ker
Spring Hope'	Til' ler y	Whit' ti er
Stain' back	Tois' not	Wil' liams bo ro
Sta' ley	Tuck a see' gee	Wil' ton
Stan' hope	Tus co' la	Win' der
Stan' tons burg	U wha' rie	Win' fall
Stone' wall	Vance	Win' na bow
Straits	Van' de mere	Win' nie
Sun' bury	Vaughan	Wrights' ville
Sup ply'	Wake field'	Yeates' ville
Swan na no' a	Wake For' est	York' ville
Swans' bo ro	War' ren Plains	Youngs' ville
Syl' va	War' saw	Zach' a ry

MOUNTAINS, RIVERS, BAYS AND SOUNDS.

LESSON 61.

MOUNTAINS.

Blue Ridge	Hi bri′ ten	Rip′ shin
Grand′ fa ther	Ta′ ble Rock	Bald
Pi′ lot	Hick′ o ry Nut	Dome
Tyr′ rell	Black Broth′ ers	Crag′ gy
U whar′ rie	Hair′ y Beard	Mitch′ ell
O co nee′ che	Roan	Grand′ moth er
Crow′ der	Bal′ sam	Hog Back
Kings	Pis′ gah	Smo′ ky
Brush′ y	Cling′ man's Dome	Guy ot′
South	New Found	Cat a loo′ che
So′ co	Cow ee′	Nan ta ha la′
Stans′ bu ry	Beau′ catch er	Lick′ stone
I′ da	Try′ on	Stone
Bend′ ing	Blow′ ing Rock	Chim′ ney
Shin′ ing Rock	Bald′ face	Hy′ der
Ju na lus′ ka	Ser′ bal	Cæ′ sar's Head

LESSON 62.

RIVERS.

Swan na no′ a	French Broad′	Ten nes see′
Tuck a see′ gee	Wa tau′ ga	Hi a was′ se
Nan ta ha la′	Che o′ wee	Val′ ley
Elk	O co na luf′ tee	New
Pig′ eon	Toe	Lin′ ville
Johns	Lit′ tle	Ca taw′ ba

LESSON 63.

RIVERS.

Green	Broad	San tee
Red' dies	Roar' ing	El' kin
Mitch' ell	Fish	Ar a rat'
Yad' kin	U whar' rie	Rock' y
Pee' Dee	Haw	Deep
Black	South	North East
Cape Fear'	Flat	E no'
Trent	Neuse	Pam' li co
Pun' go	Tar	Pan te' go
Bay	Long' Shoal	Not' ta way
Me her' rin	Chow an'	Pot e ca' si
Cat a wis' ky	A hos' kie	Pas quo tank'
Per quim' ans	Yeo pim'	Cash ie'
North	Al li ga' tor	Roan oke'

LESSON 64.

BAYS AND SOUNDS.

Ma' yo	Smith	Top' sail
New' port	White Oak	Cur ri tuck'
Al be marle'	Pam' li co	Bogue
Stump	Core	Ons' low
Cro a tan'	Ma' son bo ro	Ye sock' ing
Wrights' ville	Roan oke'	Rose
Ral' eigh	Shal' low Bay	Cath' a rine
Kit' ty hawk	Ju' ni per	Mat ta mus keet'
E' den ton	Ger' man town	Wac ca maw'
Stum' py Point	Thor' ough fare	

WOODS, TIMBERS AND SHRUBS OF NORTH CAROLINA.

LESSON 65.

Al' der	Beech	Ca tal' pa
Ap' ple	Birch	Ce' dar
Ar' bor vi' tæ	Bit' ter sweet	Cher' ry
Ar' row wood	Black' ber ry	Chest' nut
Ash	Blad' der nut	Chi' na root
As' pen	Buck' eye	Chi' na tree
Bal' sam	Buck' thorn	Chin' qua pin
Bam' boo	Buf' fa lo tree	Choke' ber ry
Bar' ber ry	Burn' ing bush	Cof' fee tree
Bay	But' ton bush	Cor' al ber ry
Bear' ber ry	But' ton wood	Cot' ton tree
Bear' grass	Cane	Cran' ber ry

LESSON 66.

Vir gin' i a creep' er	Fet' ter bush	Haz' el nut
Cross' vine	Fir	Black' haw
Cu' cum ber tree	Flow' er ing moss	Red' haw
Cur' rant	Fringe' tree	False' heath
Cy' press	Gall' ber ry	Hem' lock spruce
Deer' ber ry	Goose' ber ry	Hick' o ry
Dev' il wood	Grape	Hob' ble bush
Dew' ber ry	Ground' sel	Hol' ly
Dog' wood	Black gum	Hon' ey suck le
El' der	Sweet gum	Hop' tree
Elm	Hack' ber ry	Horn' beam
Sweet' fern	Hard' hack	Huck' le ber ry

LESSON 67.

WOODS, TIMBERS AND SHRUBS.

Hy dran' ge a	Mis' tle toe	Pep' per bush
I' ron wood	Mock or' ange	Sweet pep' per
I' vy	Moon' seed	Per sim' mon
Jes' sa mine	Moose wood	Pine
Lau' rel	Mul' ber ry	Pla' ner tree
Lea' ther wood	Myr' tle	Plum
Lime' tree	Nine' bark	Poi' son oak
Linn' tree	Oak	Poi' son vine
Lo' cust	Oil' nut	Pond' bush
Loose' strife	Pal met' to	Pri' vet
Mag no' li a	Pa paw'	Rasp' ber ry
Ma' ple	Moun' tain pep' per	Rat tan'

LESSON 68.

Red' bud	Spice' bush	Tooth' ache tree
Red' root	Spruce	Tu' lip tree
Reed	Stag' ger bush	Um' brel la tree
Rock' rose	Straw' ber ry bush	Vir' gin's bow er
Rose	Su' mach	Wal' nut
Sar sa pa ril' la	Sup' ple Jack	Witch ha' zel
Sas' sa fras	Sweet' bri er	Wild gin' ger
Ser' vice tree	Sweet' shrub	Wil' low
Sheep' ber ry	Syc' a more	Win' ter green
Sloe	Sy rin' ga	Wood' bine
Snow' drop tree	Thorn tree	Yel' low root
Sour' wood	Trail' ing arbu' tus	Yel' low wood
Spar' kle ber ry	Trum' pet flow' er	Yo' pon

MINERALS OF NORTH CAROLINA.

LESSON 69.

Gold	Stib' nite	Pyr' rho tite
Sil' ver	Bis' muth in ite	Schrei' ber site
Cop' per	Tet ra' dym ite	Pyr' ite
Plat' i num	Mo lyb' de nite	Chal' co pyr ite
I' ron	Ar' gent ite	Barn' hardt ite
Pal la' di um	Ga' len ite	Mar' cas ite
Lead	Al' ta ite	Leu cop' y rite
An' ti mo ny	Born' ite	Ar sen op' y rite
Sul' phur	Spha' ler ite	Nag' ya gite
Di' a mond	Chal' co cite	Cov' ell ite
Graph' ite	Tro' il ite	Tet ra he' drite

LESSON 70.

Ha' lite	Cas sit' er ite	Wad
Flu' or ite	U ran' in ite	Se nar mon' tite
Cu' prite	Ru' tile	Bis' mite
Me lac' on ite	An' a tase	Mo lyb' dite
Cor' un dum	Brook' ite	Quartz
Hem' a tite	Pyr o hi' site	O' pal
Me nac' can ite	Di' as pore	En' sta tite
Spi nel'	Goth' ite	Py rox' ene
Gahn' ite	Lim' on ite	Spod' u mene
Mag' net ite	Gum' mite	Hid' den ite
Chro' mite	Psi lom' e lane	Am' phi bole

LESSON 71.

MINERALS.

Horn' blende

As best' os

Ber' yl

Chrys' o lite

Gar' net

Zir' con

Ve su' vi an ite

Ep' i dote

Al' lan ite

Zo' is ite

Phlo' go pite

Cer' o lite

Mi' ca

Bi' o tite

Mus' cov ite

Feld' spar

Lab' ra dor ite

An' des ite

Ol' i go clase

Al' bite

Or' tho clase

Tour' ma line

Cy' an ite (*ky' an ite*)

Pro' chlo rite

Fi' bro lite

To' paz

Ti' tan ite

Staur' o lite

Chrys o col' la

Cal' a mine

Talc

Py roph' yl lite

Glau' con ite

Ser' pen tine

Dew' ey lite

Col' um bite

LESSON 72.

Genth' ite

Ka' o lin

Ka' o lin ite

Hal loy' site

Cul sa gee' ite

Kerr' ite

Ma' con ite

Lu' cas ite

Chlo' rite

Pen' nin ite

Pseu do mal' a chite

Scor' o dite

Chlo' ri toid

Will' cox ite

Mar' gar ite

Dud' ley ite

U ran' o til

Au' er lite

Xan' thi tane

Pyr' o chlore

Hatch et to lite

Tan' ta lite

Cu pro' scheel ite

Stolz' ite

Sa mar' skite

Fer' gus on ite

Pol' y crase

Rog' ers ite

Xen' o time

Ap' a tite

Pyr o morph' ite

Mon' az ite

Vi' vi an ite

Laz' u lite

Cal' cite

Dol' o mite

LESSON 73.

MINERALS.

Wa' vell ite	Bar' ite	Mag' nes ite
Phar ma cos id' er ite	An' gle site	Sid' er ite
Du fren' ite	Cro' co ite	Rho' do chros ite
Phos' phur an yl ite	Me lan' ter ite	Ce' russ ite
Au' tuu ite	Gos' lar ite	Mal' a chite $\,$↜
Ni' ter	Chal' canth ite	Az' u rite
Wol' fram ite	A lun' o gen	Bis' muth ite
Am' ber	Mi' sy	An' thra cite
Scheel' ite	Mon' tan ite	Lig' nite

FAMILY NAMES IN NORTH CAROLINA HISTORY.

LESSON 74.

Ad' ams	Av' e ry	Berke' ley
Alex an' der	Bad' ger	Ber' ry
Al' len	Ba' ker	Blake' ly
Al' ston	Bain	Black' ledge
Al' der man	Barnes	Blair
An' drews	Barn' well	Black' nall
An' der son	Bar' rin ger	Blood' worth
Arm' strong	Bat' tle	Blount
Ashe	Beas' ley	Boone
Ash' ley	Ben' bu ry	Bow' er
At' kin son	Ben' nett	Boy' lan
Av' e ra	Ber nard'	Boyd

LESSON 75.

FAMILY NAMES IN NORTH CAROLINA.

Boy′ kin	Burke	Cas′ well
Bragg	Bur′ kett	Cher′ ry
Branch	Bur′ ton	Clark
Bre vard′	But′ ler	Clarke
Brick′ ell	Bur′ well	Cleve′ land
Briggs	By′ num	Cling′ man
Brown	Cald′ well	Cobb
Bry′ an	Cam′ e ron	Cog′ dell
Brog′ den	Camp′ bell	Coke
Bunn	Cant′ well	Col′ lins
Bur′ gess	Ca′ rey	Con′ nor
Bur gwyn′	Carr	Cook

LESSON 76.

Cor nell′	Da′ vid son	Dowd
Cot′ ten	Da′ vis	Drake
Cowles	Den′ son	Drum′ mond
Cox	De Ros set′ (*Der o zet′*)	Dud′ ley
Craig	Dev′ er eux	Du rant′
Cra′ ven	Dick′ en son	Ea′ ton
Craw′ ford	Dick′ in son	E′ den
Cru′ dup	Dob′ bin	El′ lis
Dan′ iel	Dobbs	Ed′ mund son
Dan′ iels	Don′ nell	Ed′ wards
Da′ vie	Don′ nell son	En′ gel hard
Daves	Down′ ing	Ev′ er ard

LESSON 77.

FAMILY NAMES IN NORTH CAROLINA.

Fai' son	Fur' man	Glov' er
Fan' ning	Gale	Gor' don
Far' mer	Gales	Gra' dy
Fer' gus on	Gal' lo way	De Graf' fen reid
Fin' ger	Gar' rett	Gra' ham
Fitts	Gas' ton	Gran' dy
Fish' er	Gates	Greene
Flem' ing	Gat' ling	Greg' o ry
Fol' some	Ged' dy	Grims' ley
Fowle	Gil les' pie	Grimes
Frank' lin	Gil' liam	Gui' on
Fray	Glas' gow	Hall

LESSON 78.

Ham' il ton	Hawks	Hogg
Han' cock	Haw' kins	Hoke
Hard' ing	Hay	Hol' den
Har' dy	Hay' wood	Holmes
Har' gett	Heartt	Holt
Har' grove	Heart	Hoop' er
Har' nett	Hen' der son	How' ard
Har' ris	Hen' ry	Howe
Har' vey	Hewes	How' ell
Har' rell	Hill	Hughes
Has' sell	Hines	Hunt
Hale	Hodg' son	Hun' ter

LESSON 79.

FAMILY NAMES IN NORTH CAROLINA.

Hus' bands	Ke' nan	Leak
Hyde	Kerr	Lee
Ire' dell	Kings' bu ry	Leigh
Ives	King	Le noir'
In' nes	Kitch' in	Les' lie
Jar' vis	La Fay' ette	Lew' is
Jer' ni gan	Lamb	Lil' ling ton
Joc' e lyn	Lane	Lit' tle
John' ston	La' tham	Locke
John' son	Law' son	Lock' hart
Jones	Lea	Lon' don
Joy' ner	Leach	Long

LESSON 80.

Love' joy	Mc Bryde'	Mc Lean'
Lowe	Mc Don' ald	Mc Leod'
Low' rie	Mc Dow' ell	Mc Neill'
Lud' well	Mc Far' land	Mac Rae'
Lyt' tle	Mc Ge' hee	Meares
Ma' con	Mc Gee'	Meb' ane
Man' gum	Mc Guire'	Mer' e dith
Man' ly	Mc In tyre'	Mer' ri mon
Mar' tin	Mc I' ver	Mick' el john
Mc Ad' en	Mc Kay'	Mill' er
Mc Al' lis ter	Mc Ke' than	Mitch' ell
Mc Bray' er	Mc Knight'	Mont' ford

LESSON 81.

Mont gom' er y

Moore

Mor' de cai

More' head

Mor' gan

Mor' ri son

Mor' son

Mose' ley

Mur' free

Mur' phey

Nash

No' ble

Nor' wood

Os' borne

Out' law

O' wen

Pax' ton

Pear' son

Pen' der

Pet' ti grew

Polk

Pol' lok

Pol' lock

Pot' ter

Price

Pritch' ard

Pyle

Rad' cliffe

Ral' eigh

Ram' seur

Ran' som

Ra' vens croft

Reade

Reed

Reid

Rich' ard son

LESSON 82.

Rid' dick

Rid' ley

Rob' in son

Ruf' fin

Ruth' er ford

Samp' son

San' ders

San' der lin

Satch' well

Saun' ders

Saw' yer

Scales

Scott

Sea' well

Set' tle

Shel' by

Shep' herd

Sin' gle ta ry

Sit' greaves

Skin' ner

Slings' by

Sloan

Slo' cumb

Smith

Speight

Spen' cer

Stan' ford

Stan' ly

Stark' ey

Stead' man

Stearnes

Steele

Ste' phens

Stokes

Stone

Strange

Strud' wick

Sum' ner

Sum' ter

LESSON 83.

Sut' ton	Vail	Will' iam son
Swain	Vance	Wil' son
Swann	Ven' a ble	Win' der
Tate	Wade	Wins' low
Ta' tum	Wad dell'	Win' ston
Tay' lor	Wake	Wright
Tew	Walk' er	Wood
Thomp' son	War' ren	Worth
Tip' ton	Web' ster	Worth' am
Toom' er	Well' borne	Wynns
Try' on	Whit' a ker	Wynne
Tuck' er	White	Yan' cey
Tur' ner	Whit' ford	Yeo' mans
Tyr' rell	Will' iams	Young

The foregoing list does not contain all prominent family names in North Carolina, but such as are often misspelled.

EXERCISES FOR DICTATION.

LESSON 84.

Asheville is known in North Carolina as the "Queen City of the West." It nestles charmingly among the Blue Ridge Mountains.

Raleigh is one of the most beautiful of the Southern capital cities. Its streets are wide and straight and well-shaded. The Capitol is an elegant granite structure, and cost over $500,000.

The permanent home of the North Carolina Teachers' Assembly is located at *Morehead City*, on the Atlantic Coast.

The teachers have erected there a large and commodious building for their summer meetings, which are held in June of each year.

Goldsboro is an important railroad center, and possesses many handsome residences.

Durham is the famous tobacco city of America. The product of its factories is used in every country on the globe.

New Bern was founded by Baron de Graffenreid in 1723, and named in honor of his former home, Bern, in Switzerland.

Wilmington is the sea-port metropolis of North Carolina. Vessels ply between its ports and many parts of the world.

In making a journey from *Murphy* to *Morehead City* you will pass the following county-seats: *Robbinsville, Bryson City, Waynesville, Asheville, Marion, Morganton, Newton, Statesville, Salisbury, Lexington, Greensboro, Graham, Hillsboro, Durham, Raleigh, Goldsboro, Kinston* and *New Bern*, and you would ride five hundred and eighty-five miles.

On the 20th of May, 1775, the people of *Charlotte* held a public meeting and proclaimed to the world the first declaration of independence known in America. This important event is each year celebrated in North Carolina with appropriate ceremonies.

The famous trial of the Regulators was held at *Hillsboro* in 1774.

Winston and *Salem* are separated by only a street, and they are called "The Twin Cities of North Carolina."

The "Normal and Industrial College for Young Women" is located at *Greensboro*. This institution is the result of work by the Teachers' Assembly, and is the first appropriation by North Carolina in aid of the education of the women of the State.

FAMILIAR AMERICANISMS.

These words are in general use in the current literature of the age, but they are not considered always in good taste by the best writers and speakers.

LESSON 85.

Hood' lum,	A young rowdy.
Dude,	A kind of dandy.
Boom,	Fictitious values.
Row' dy,	A ruffian.
Du dine',	Female dude.
Cau' cus,	A preliminary party meeting.
Bolt' er,	One who deserts a political party.
Lynch,	Punishment inflicted without law.
Shod' dy,	Worthless.
Bo' gus,	Not genuine.

LESSON 86.

Green' back,	National paper currency.
Spread ea' gle,	Unduly eloquent.
Loaf' er,	A lazy lounger.
Bun' combe,	Spoken for mere show.
Lob' by,	Personal influence used with legislators.
Grog' ger y,	A grog-shop.
Mile' age,	Miles traveled.
Dead beat',	A worthless idler.
Bum' mer,	One who imposes on his friends.
Drum' mer,	A traveling salesman.

LESSON 87.

Log' roll ing,	Political machinery.
Wire' pull ing,	Planning political results.
Dead' head,	Without paying.
Tramp,	A vagrant.
Bam boo' zle,	To deceive.
Dig' gings,	Locality.
Squat' ter,	To settle upon land without a title.
Mass' meet ing,	A general meeting of citizens.
Crank,	An enthusiast.
Fu' tures,	Goods bought for future delivery.
Wharf' rat,	A gamin along the wharfs.
Blab,	To tell.

LESSON 88.

Back' log,	The big log on the fire.
Back' woods,	On the frontier.
Bangs,	Curled hair on the forehead.
Be fud' dle,	Beclouded and confused.
Rat' tled,	Confused.
Black' mail,	Money extorted by threats.
Bo nan' za,	Suddenly successful.
Both' er some,	Inconvenient.
Breez' y,	Full of animation.
Bron' co,	A native California horse.
Cal' a boose,	A city jail.
Can' ner y,	Where fruit is canned.

LESSON 89.

Car' pet bag ger,	A political tramp.
Cat' nap,	A very short sleep.
Ca vort',	To frisk.
Cen ten' ni al,	The one hundredth anniversary.
Cheek' y,	Impudent.
Ca hoot',	Partnership.
Cor' ral,	To put into a close place.
Craze,	A temporary hobby.
Crook' ed,	Not honest.
Dash' y,	Showy.
Doc' tor,	To tamper with.
Ske dad' dle,	To leave suddenly.

LESSON 90.

Fad,	A trifling pursuit.
Fil i bus' ter,	To delay legislation.
Ga loot'	A worthless fellow.
Get' up,	Style of dress.
Guy,	To worry.
In' ter view,	To obtain information for publication.
Ku klux',	Southern regulators of political wrongs.
Lo' cate,	To settle.
Make' up,	General composition.
Nag,	To tease.
Nob' by,	Stylish.
Queer,	Counterfeit money.

LESSON 91.

Shys' ter,	A trickish fellow.
Skimp' y,	Parsimonious saving.
Snap,	Energy.
So' cia ble,	An informal party.
Sport,	A gambler.
Crook,	A burglar.
Ta boo',	To dishonor.
Vim,	Energy.
Get there,	To be successful.
Pal,	A partner in crime.
Green goods,	Counterfeit money.
Bear,	One who reduces prices of stocks.
Bull,	One who advances prices of stocks.

FAMILIAR ABBREVIATIONS.

Abbreviations generally indicate carelessness in writing, and they should never be used except when absolutely necessary.

LESSON 92.

A. or Ans. Answer.

A. B. or B. A. Bachelor of Arts.

A. B. S. American Bible Society.

A. C. or B. C. Before Christ.

Acc. or Acct. Account.

A. D. In the year of our Lord.

Æ. or Æt. Of age; aged.

Ala. Alabama.

Alex. Alexander.

A. M. Master of Arts; Before noon; In the year of the world.

A. & M. Col. Agricultural and Mechanical College.

Am. American.

Anon. Anonymous.

Apr. April.

Ark. Arkansas.

A. A. Arizona Territory.

Att. or Atty. Attorney

Aug. August.

Bbl. Barrel; Barrels.

B. D. Bachelor of Divinity.

Bp. Bishop.

C. or Cent. A hundred.

Cal. California; Calendar.

Capt. Captain.

LESSON 93.

Cash. Cashier.
C. E. Civil Engineer.
Ch. Church; Chapter; Charles.
C. J. Chief Justice.
Co. Company; County.
Col. Colonel.
Coll. College; Collector.
Colo. Colorado.
Cong. Congress.
Conn. or Ct. Connecticut.
Const. Constable; Constitution.
C. S. A. Confederate States of America.

Cr. Credit or Creditor.
Cts. Cents.
Cwt. A hundred weight.
Dan. Daniel.
D. C. District of Columbia.
D. D. Doctor of Divinity.
Dea. Deacon.
Dec. December.
Del. Delaware; Delegate.
Dist. District.
Do. Ditto; the same.
Doz. Dozen.
Dr. Debtor; Doctor; Dram.

LESSON 94.

E. East; Eastern.
Ed. Edition; Editor.
E. G. For example.
Eng. England; English.
Esq. or Esqr. Esquire.
Etc. or &c. And so forth.
Exc. Excellency.
F. A. M. Free and Accepted Masons.
Feb. February.
Fig. Figure; Figures.
Fla. Florida.
Fr. France; Francis; French.
Fri. Friday.

F. R. S. Fellow of the Royal Society.
F. S. A. Fellow of the Society of Arts, or of Antiquaries.
Ga. Georgia.
Gen. General; Genesis.
Gent. Gentlemen.
Gov. Governor.
H. B. M. His or Her Britannic Majesty.
Hhd. Hogshead; Hogsheads.
Hist. History; Historical.
Hon. Honorable.
H. R. House of Representatives.

LESSON 95.

H. S. S. Fellow of the Historical Society.

Hund. Hundred; Hundreds.

Ib. or Ibid. In the same place.

Id. The same.

Id. T. Idaho Territory.

I. e. That is.

I. H. S. Jesus Saviour of men.

Ill. Illinois.

Incog. Unknown.

Ind. Indiana; India; Indian.

Ind. T. Indian Territory.

Inst. Instant—the present month.

Int. Interest.

Io. Iowa.

I. O. O. F. Independent Order of Odd Fellows.

It. Italian; Italy.

J. Judge.

Jan. January.

Jas. James.

Jno. John.

Jos. Joseph.

J. P. Justice of the Peace.

Jr. or Jun. Junior.

Kan. Kansas.

K. P. Knights of Pythias.

L., l. or £. A pound sterling.

La. Louisiana.

Lat. Latin; Latitude.

LESSON 96.

Leg. or Legis. Legislature.

Lieut. or Lt. Lieutenant.

LL. D. Doctor of Laws.

Lon. Longitude; London.

L. S. Place of the Seal.

M. Marquis; Monsieur; Mile; Morning; Noon; Thousand.

Maj. Major.

Mass. Massachusetts.

Math. Mathematics.

M. C. Member of Congress.

M. D. Doctor of Physic.

Md. Maryland.

Me. Maine.

Messrs. Gentlemen; Sirs.

Mich. Michigan.

Minn. Minnesota.

Miss. or Mi. Mississippi.

Mo. Missouri; Mouth.

Mon. Monday.

M. P. Member of Parliament.

Mr. Mister.

Mrs. Mistress.

MS. Manuscript.

Mt. Mount or Mountain.

M. T. Montana Territory.

N. North.

N. A. North America.

LESSON 97.

N. B.   Take Notice.

N. C.   North Carolina.

N. D.   North Dakota.

N. C. S. G.   North Carolina State Guard.

N. C. T. A.   North Carolina Teachers' Assembly.

N. E.   North-east; New England.

N. E. A.   National Educational Association.

Neb.   Nebraska.

Nev.   Nevada.

N. H.   New Hampshire.

N. J.   New Jersey.

N. M.   New Mexico.

No.   Number.

N. O.   New Orleans.

Nov.   November.

N. S.   Nova Scotia.

N. T.   New Testament.

N. W.   North-west.

N. Y.   New York.

O.   Ohio.

Ob.   (*Obiit.*) Died.

Oct.   October.

On. or Or.   Oregon.

O. T.   Old Testament.

Oz.   Ounce or Ounces.

Pa. or Penn.   Pennsylvania.

Per or pr.   By the; as, *per* yard.

LESSON 98.

Per ct.   By the hundred.

Ph. D.   Doctor of Philosophy.

P. M.   Postmaster; Afternoon.

P. O.   Post-office.

Pres.   President; Present.

Prof.   Professor.

Pro tem.   For the time being.

Prox.   Next month.

P. S.   Postscript; Privy Seal.

Ps.   Psalm; Psalms.

Pub.   Public; Publisher.

Pub. Doc.   Public Documents.

Q.   Query; Question; Queen.

Q. L.   As much as you please.

Q. M. G.   Quartermaster General.

Q. S.   A sufficient quantity.

Qt.   Quart; Quantity.

Q. V.   As much as you please; Which see.

Rec. Sec.   Recording Secretary.

Rep.   Representative; Republican.

Rev.   Revelations; Reverend.

R. I.   Rhode Island.

Robt.   Robert.

R. R.   Railroad; Right Reverend.

Rt. Hon.   Right Honorable.

S.   South.

S. A.   South America.

LESSON 99.

Sam. Samuel.

Sat. Saturday.

S. C. South Carolina.

Sc. or Sculp. (*Sculpsit.*) He, or she, engraved it.

S. D. South Dakota.

S. E. South-east.

S. E. A. Southern Educational Association.

Sec. Secretary; Section.

Sen. Senate; Senator.

Sept. September.

Serg. Sergeant.

Sr. Sir; Senior.

SS. Namely; Half.

Sun. Sunday.

S. S. Sunday-school.

S. W. South-west.

T. Town; Territory; Ton.

Tenn. Tennessee.

Tex. Texas.

Th. or Thos. Thomas.

Thurs. Thursday.

Tr. Treasurer; Trustee.

Tu. or Tues. Tuesday.

Ult. Last, or the last month.

U. S. A. United States of America; United States Army.

U. S. M. United States Marine; United States Mail.

LESSON 100.

U. S. United States.

U. S. M. A. United States Military Academy.

U. S. N. United States Navy.

U. S. S. United States Senate.

U. T. Utah Territory.

V. (*Vide.*) See; Verse.

Va. Virginia.

Viz. Namely; To-wit.

Vol. or vol. Volume.

V. P. Vice-President.

Vt. Vermont.

W. West.

W. C. T. U. Woman's Christian Temperance Association.

Wis. Wisconsin.

W. Washington.

W. Va. West Virginia.

Wy. T. Wyoming Territory.

X. or Xt. Christ.

Xm. or Xmas. Christmas.

Xn. or Xtian. Christian.

Y. or Yr. Year.

Yd. or yd. Yard.

Y. M. C. A. Young Men's Christian Association.

Y. P. S. C. E. Young People's Society of Christian Endeavor.

Z. G. Zoological Garden.

Zool. Zoology.

FORMS OF LETTERS AND COMMERCIAL PAPERS.

LESSON 101.

AN ORDER FOR BOOKS.

ASHEVILLE, N. C., August 1, 1892.

MESSRS. ALFRED WILLIAMS & CO.,
Raleigh, N. C.

GENTLEMEN:—Please forward to me by first Express

24 North Carolina Spelling-books.

12 Spencer's First Steps in North Carolina History.

12 Moore's School History of North Carolina.

27 North Carolina Copy-books, $\frac{6}{1}$, $\frac{4}{2}$, 3, $\frac{2}{4}$, 5, 6, $\frac{3}{7}$, $\frac{2}{8}$, 9.

and oblige,　　　　　　　Yours truly,

(MISS) MARY A. JONES.

LESSON 102.

NOTE.

$100.00.　　　　　GREENVILLE, N. C., January 1, 1892.

Twelve months after date I promise to pay to the order of Thomas H. Robertson One Hundred Dollars, with interest at six per cent. per annum, for value received.

GEORGE W. WASHINGTON.

SIGHT DRAFT.

$44.$\frac{20}{100}$　　　　WILMINGTON, N. C., September 1, 1892.

At sight pay to the order of John T. Smith Forty-four and $\frac{20}{100}$ Dollars, and charge to my account.

ROBERT G. DUNN.

To MR. W. G. BARNES,
Greensboro, N. C.

LESSON 103.

A FAMILY LETTER.

CHARLOTTE, N. C., May 20, 1775.

DEAR BROTHER HENRY:—There is great excitement in this little village of Charlotte to-day. Late yesterday afternoon a courier, riding all the way from Boston, brought news that the British soldiers had fired upon the Americans at Lexington on April 19th. The people here are aroused as never before. A great crowd assembled last night in a large room and Mr. Abraham Alexander presided over the meeting. After remaining in session all night, speaking and consulting, Dr. Ephraim Brevard drew up some strong resolutions, declaring that North Carolina would hereafter be independent of Great Britain forever. Everybody voted for the resolutions, and when they were read in the public square to-day the people cheered as if they were wild and endorsed the bold declaration of independence.

I wonder how King George will like that.

Your affectionate brother,

PAUL JONES.

LESSON 104.

RECEIPT.

$2,317.$\frac{99}{100}$ WILSON, N. C., June 12, 1892.

Received of Mrs. Mary H. Paywell Twenty-three Hundred and Seventeen and $\frac{99}{100}$ Dollars, in full of account to date.

ROBERT MORRIS & CO.

DUE BILL.

$325.$\frac{50}{100}$ ROANOKE ISLAND, N. C., October 19, 1892.

Due on demand, to Christopher Columbus, Three Hundred and Twenty-five and $\frac{50}{100}$ Dollars, value received.

WALTER RALEIGH.

LESSON 105.

BILL AND RECEIPT.

GREENSBORO, N. C., July 5, 1892.

MR. ALEXANDER HARRIS,

To WALTER THOMPSON, *Dr.*

1892. July	1	To tuition of Henry, 2d quarter......................	$ 10	00	
		" " " Mary, 2d quarter..........	10	00	
		" " " " in music.....................	5	00	
		" use of Piano for practice......................	1	50	
					$ 26 50

Received payment,

WALTER THOMPSON.

July 10, 1892.

ORDER FOR MERCHANDISE.

JULY 4, 1892.

MESSRS. BROWN & JONES:

Please deliver to Robert Workman, or order, merchandise such as he may desire to the amount of Fifty Dollars and charge to my account.

WILLIAM HOUSE.

LETTER OF CREDIT.

FAYETTEVILLE, N. C., August 12, 1892.

GENTLEMEN:—Allow me to introduce to you the bearer, Mr. John Tryman.   Should he make a selection from your stock to the amount of Three Thousand Dollars, I will be answerable for that sum in case of his non-payment.   ·   Yours truly,

WRIGHT RICH.

To MESSRS. B. D. BARKER & CO.,

New York.

PRACTICE WORDS.

LESSON 106.

in flam' ma ble
in sep' a ra ble
i ras' ci ble
ir re triev' a ble
su prem' a cy
mil' lin er y
mil' i ta ry
con sci en' tious
em bar' rass ment
con va les' cent
ec' sta cy

em' is sa ry
aq' ue duct
dis cern' i ble
leg' a cy
dis' ci pline
ex cres' cence
ef fer vesce'
hy poth' e sis
gar' ru lous
pac' i fy
. prej' u dice

ev a nes' cent
par' al lel
co a lesce'
bel lig' er ent
il leg' i ble
mar' i ner
in er' ti a
con du' cive
scin' til late
sau' ci ly
cem' e te ry

LESSON 107.

pres' tige
e lic' it ed
il lit' er ate
lus' cious
in vin' ci ble
fa tigu' ing
sen' si ble
im' mi nent
pa tri' cian
bat tal' ion
con fed' er ate

ad' ju tant
strat' e gy
vac' u um
colo' nel (*kur' nel*)
ef ful' gence
prec' e dent
a cid' i ty
se ces' sion
pop' u lace
bach' e lor
pro ceed' ing

las' si tude
fas' ci nat ing
as sas' sin ate
lac' er ate
guer ril' la
ob lique'
ab er ra' tion
col lis' ion
co er' cion
min' i a ture
pi' quan cy

LESSON 108.

ca rouse'
ca tas' tro phe
cau' cus
cha' os
charge' a ble
chi me' ra
chiv' al ry
chyle
chyme
cic' a trice
clique
co' coa

col' league
col lo' qui al
comb
com plai' sance
con' duit
con dign'
con va lesce'
con vey'
corps
coun' ter feit
cou' ri er
court' e sy

corpse
cous' in
cox' comb
croup
cruise
crumb
crypt
cuck' oo
cu' po la
de fi' cient
dem' a gogue
di' a logue

LESSON 109.

dil' i gence
dis guise'
di shev' el
dom' i cile
dough' ty
dys' en ter y
dys pep' si a
ea' gle
ef fer vesce'
e lec tri' cian
el' e phant
en cy clo pe' di a

en fran' chise
e ques' tri an
er y sip' e las
es' pi on age
ex cru' ci ate
ex haust'
fa tigue'
fic ti' tious
flaunt
com' par a ble
com plex' ion
sac' ri fice

cor rob' o rate
am a ran' thine
arch' i tect
de clam' a to ry
in dis sol' u ble
par' al yze
stell' u lar
tal' is man
ad o les' cence
cui rass'
ex ag' ger ate
a nath' e ma

LESSON 110.

o bei′ sauce

skep′ ti cism

chro nol′ o gy

ex quis′ ite

a bridg′ ment

hein′ ous

lab′ y rinth

ca pac′ i ty

in dict′ ment

cal′ en dar

del′ i ble

cha lyb′ e ate

con niv′ ance

dy′ nas ty

e piph′ a ny

dis pen′ sa ry

res′ er voir

flo res′ cence

for bade′

for′ eign er

fran′ chise

fric as see′

fur′ lough

gay′ e ty

gauge

ga zelle′

ghast′ ly

ghost

ghoul

gi raffe′

gla′ cier

gnarled

go′ pher

gor′ geous

gour′ mand

grand′ eur

LESSON 111.

gro tesque′

guar an tee′

guar′ an ty

gud′ geon

guil′ lo tine

guin′ ea

guise

gyp′ sy

hearth

heif′ er

heir′ loom

hem′ i sphere

12

herb′ age

hi e ro glyph′ ic

hoax

hough

how′ itz er

hos′ tler

hy′ a cinth

hy e′ na

hy per′ bo la

ice′ berg

ich neu′ mon

ich thy ol′ o gy

i′ ci cle

i′ dyl

im′ be cile

in dig′ e nous

in gen′ ious

in trigu′ er

i′ o dide

i ras′ ci ble

jas′ mine

jeop′ ard y

jave′ lin

jour′ ney

LESSON 112.

ju di′ cious

jui′ cy

ka lei′ do scope

kan ga roo′

knick′ knack

lab′ y rinth

lar′ ynx

lic′ o rice

lieu ten′ ant

li tig′ ious

loath′ some

lunch′ eon

lux u′ ri ance

lynx

ma chine′

Ma dei′ ra

ma gi′ cian

mal fea′ sance

ma li′ cious

ma lign′

man′ a cle

man eu′ ver

ma′ ny

mar′ riage

mea′ sles

mè′ di o cre

mer′ can tile

me ri′ no

met a mor′ phose

mi as′ ma

mi li′ tia

mill′ ion aire

mis′ chief

mis′ sion a ry

moi′ e ty

mon′ eys

LESSON 113.

mon′ eyed

mort′ gage

mor′ tise

mus tache′

mus′ cle

mu si′ cian

mus qui′ to

naph′ tha

ne go′ ti ate

neigh′ bor hood

neu ral′ gi a

nymph

o bei′ sance

of fi′ cious

o′ gre

om nis′ cient

o′ nyx

op ti′ cian

or′ phan

pæ′ an

pag′ eant ry

pan e gyr′ ic

par′ al yze

par′ ox ysm

pa′ tri arch

pe cul′ iar

peo′ ple

pe riph′ e ry

per ni′ cious

per suade′

pha′ e ton

phys′ ic

phys i og′ no my

phy sique′

pi az′ za

pict ur esque′

LESSON 114.

pig' eon

pom' ace

por' phy ry

prai' rie

pre co' cious

pro dig' ious

pro fi' cien cy

proph' e cy

pur' lieus

pyr o tech' nics

quar tette'

quay

qui' nine

quoit

rasp' ber ry

reck' on

rec on noi' ter

re cruit'

rhap' so dy

rheu' ma tism

rhi noc' e ros

rhu' barb

rhyme

ro' guish

ru ta ba' ga

sa' ti ate

scal' lop

scar la ti' na

scim' i ter

scis' sors

scourge

scythe

sen' su al

shrewd

sil' hou ette

sluice

LESSON 115.

sol' dier

souve' nir

sov' er eign

spe' cies

sphe' roid

sphinx

stat' u ette

ste' re o type

stom' ach

su per fi' cial

sur' feit

tab. leau'

tam bour ine'

tech' nic al

tur quois'

ty' phoid

u nique'

val' iant

va lise'

vex a' tious

vil' lain ous

vi' ti ate

weird

wres' tle

wretch' ed

yacht

bac cha na' li an

bru nette'

chan de lier'

ca tarrh'

co quette'

cro quet'

dis' tich

e clat'

el ee mos' y na ry

e lite'

LESSON 116.

en nui'
et i quette'
gher' kin
gym na' si um
hic' cough
ho' sier y
id i o syn' cra sy
nau' seous
neph' ew
phlegm
ac ces' so ry
rec i proc' i ty

psy chol' o gy
queue
ra' ti o
sap o na' ceous
aid' de camp
bay' ou
belles let' tres
bil' let doux
blanc mange'
brag ga do' ci o
am' a teur
am' e thyst

buoy' an cy
cham pagne'
caout' chouc
carte blanche'
con' science
da guerre' o type
dah' lia
de bris'
dis cern' i ble
en core'
basque
ba zaar'

LESSON 117.

co erce'
pros' e lyte
mad em oi selle'
mag ne' si a
men ag' e rie
mign on ette'
nau' se ate
pen i ten' tia ry
port man' teau
tech' nic al
ad' u la to ry
ces sa' tion

judg' ment
pro ced' ure
right' eous
ser' geant
sub' tle ty
vign ette'
bour geois'
gaug' ing
zeph' yr
an' al yze
an' o dyne
an' swer

ed' i fice
sub ter ra' ne ous
har angue'
be leag' uer
cor' ol la ry
guil' lo tine
a poc' ryph al
souve' nir
dis syl' la ble
bea' con
beau
bis' cuit

www.ingramcontent.com/pod-product-compliance
Lightning Source LLC
Chambersburg PA
CBHW020538270326
41927CB00006B/629